SUCCESSFUL CHILDREN, SUCCESSFUL TEACHING

Enriching the primary curriculum: child, teacher, context

Series editor: Janet Moyles

The series highlights some of the major challenges and issues which face teachers on a day-to-day basis in handling their apparently ever widening roles in primary schools. Curriculum experiences can, and should be enriching and stimulating for everyone but there must be a recognition and appreciation of the crucial interface between child, teacher and the context of school and society, rather than a focus on mere curriculum 'delivery'.

Each volume in the series seeks to enrich and extend readers' curriculum thinking beyond the current narrow confines through recognizing and celebrating the very essence of what makes primary teaching demanding but exciting, creative, dynamic and, yes, even enjoyable! The series recognizes that at the heart of teaching lies children and that 'subjects' are merely tools towards enabling an education which develops both understanding and enthusiasm for life-long learning.

The authors' underpinning, integrated rationale is to enable teachers to analyse their own practices by exploring those of others through cameos of real life events taken from classroom and school contexts. The aim throughout is to help teachers regain their sense of ownership over changes to classroom and curricular practices and to develop an enhanced and enriched understanding of theory through practice.

Current and forthcoming titles:

Florence Beetlestone: *Creative children, imaginative teaching*
Max de Boo: *Enquiring children, challenging teaching*
Deirdre Cook and Helen Finlayson: *Interactive children, constructive teaching*
Roger Merry: *Successful children, successful teaching*
Janet Moyles: *Playful children, inspired teaching*
Wendy Suschitzky and Joy Chapman: *Valued children, informed teaching*
Jill Williams: *Independent children, sensitive teaching*

SUCCESSFUL CHILDREN, SUCCESSFUL TEACHING

Roger Merry

Open University Press
Buckingham • Philadelphia

Open University Press
Celtic Court
22 Ballmoor
Buckingham
MK18 1XW

and
1900 Frost Road, Suite 101
Bristol, PA 19007, USA

First Published 1998

A catalogue record of this book is available from the British Library

ISBN   0 335 19743 4 (hb)   0 335 19742 6 (pb)

Library of Congress Cataloging-in-Publication Data
Merry. Roger.
    Successful children, successful teaching / by Roger Merry.
        p.   cm. — (Enriching the primary curriculum—child,
    teacher, context)
    Includes bibliographical references and index.
    ISBN 0–335–19743–4. — ISBN 0–335–19742–6 (pbk.)
    1. Elementary school teaching. 2. Learning, Psychology of.
3. Cognition.   I. Title.   II. Series.
LB1666.M487 1997
372.1102—dc21   97–17212
                                                                      CIP

Typeset by Graphicraft Typesetters Ltd, Hong Kong
Printed in Great Britain by St Edmundsbury Press Ltd,
Bury St Edmunds, Suffolk

Contents

Series editor's preface

Cameo

Glenn has taught across the age range in different primary schools for the last 15 years, specializing in art. In that time, he has had to make many adjustments in his thinking. The emphasis now appears to have shifted significantly from considering the learning needs of children as paramount, to 'delivering' a curriculum over which he feels little ownership and about which he feels even less real enthusiasm! The National Curriculum, with its individual subjects and language of 'teaching', not to mention an impending Office for Standards in Education (Ofsted) inspection, has shaken his confidence somewhat in his own understanding of what primary education is all about. It has also meant that he feels *he* is doing most of the learning, rather than the children – all those detailed plans and topic packs for individual subjects which teachers have been developing within the school seem to Glenn to leave little for children to actually do except explore the occasional artefact and fill in worksheets.

Yet he knows that he enjoys the 'buzz' of teaching, revels in being part of children's progress and achievements, delights in those rare times when he can indulge in art activities with children, is appreciated by parents and colleagues for the quality of his work and, generally, still finds his real heart lies in being an educator and doing something worthwhile. His constant question to himself is 'How can I work with children in ways I feel and *know* are appropriate and yet meet the outside demands made on me?'

Sound familiar? You may well begin to recognize a 'Glenn' within you! He encapsulates the way many teachers are feeling at the present time and the persistent doubts and uncertainties which continually underpin many teacher's work. In the early and middle years of primary schooling in particular, teachers are facing great challenges in conceiving how best to accommodate the learning needs of children in a context of growing pressure, innovation and subject curriculum demand. Yet conscientiousness drives the professional to strive for greater understanding – that little bit more knowledge or skill might just make a big difference to one child or it might provide improved insights into one aspect of the curriculum.

Glenn, like many teachers, needs time, encouragement and support to reflect on his current practice and to consider in an objective way the changes needed. Rather than trying to add something else to an already overcrowded curriculum, today's teachers should consider those existing aspects which are fundamental to ensuring that children are not only schooled but educated in the broadest possible sense. Only then can we begin to sort out those things which are vital, those things we would like to do and those things which would benefit from a rethink.

This series aims to offer practitioners food for thought as well as practical and theoretical support in establishing, defining and refining their own understandings and beliefs. It focuses particularly on enriching curriculum experiences for everyone through recognizing and appreciating the crucial interface between the child, the teacher and the context of primary education, including the curriculum context. Each title in the series seeks collectively and individually to enhance teachers' understanding about the theories which underpin, guide and enrich quality practice in a range of broader curriculum aspects, whilst acknowledging issues such as class size and overload, common across primary schools today.

Each book operates from the basis of exploring teachers' sound – frequently intuitive – experiences and understanding of teaching and learning processes and outcomes, which most teachers inevitably possess in good measure and which, like Glenn, they often feel constrained to use. For example, the editor is regularly told by teachers and others in primary schools that they 'know' or 'feel' that play for children is or must be a valuable process, yet they are also aware that this is not often reflected in their planning or curriculum management, and that the context of education generally is antithetical to play. What is more, they really do not know what to do about it and find articulating the justification for play practices extremely difficult. Other writers in the series have suggested that this is also the case in their areas of expertise.

All the books in this series seek to enrich and extend teachers' curriculum thinking beyond the level of just 'subjects', into dimensions related to the teaching and learning needs of children and the contextual demands faced by schools. The books cover areas such as creativity, success and competence, exploration and problem-solving, information technology across subjects and boundaries, play in the primary curriculum, questioning and teacher–child interactions, values in relation to equality issues, social, moral and spiritual frameworks and physical aspects of teaching and learning. Each book has had, within its working title, the rationale of the unique triad of child, teacher and context which underpins all primary schooling and education for example in this particular case, successful children and successful teaching. This has served to emphasize for authors the inextricable and imperative balance in this triad for effective classroom and curriculum practices. The model we have developed and agreed is shown below.

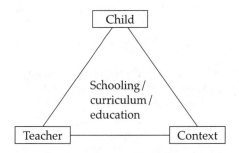

All the writers in the series have been concerned to emphasize the quality, nature and extent of existing classroom practices, and how it is possible to build on these sound pedagogical bases. For this reason, chapters within each title often begin with two or more cameos offering features of practice as starting points for teasing out aspects requiring enquiry, analysis, evaluation and discussion. Chapters then develop their own relevant themes but with consistent reference to what these mean to children and teachers within the general autonomy, and constraints, of the school context.

Issues concerning the *child* take their stance from cognitive psychology (as this book does) and include the child as:

- an active searcher after meaning;
- an individual with particular perceptions of the world and their part in it;
- a person who can reflect on their own learning and understanding;
- a learner with his or her own curriculum needs and interests to be considered;
- an interactive person, learning in collaboration with peers and adults;
- a unique individual but also one with collective needs;
- a member of a 'social' community, i.e. home, family, school, wider community.

Aspects to do with the teaching role lay stress on the *teacher* as a reflective and critical professional who will occasionally but regularly need to stand back from day-to-day practice in order to think about and analyse the triadic relationships and to acknowledge:

- their own learning styles and experiences;
- their own beliefs, values, knowledge and conceptual understanding of pedagogy;
- their need to raise questions about practice and find solutions in an ongoing way;
- their role as mutual learners with children and colleagues;
- their responsibilities as facilitators of learning, as models of learning and as negotiators of meaning with children;
- their role in enabling children's learning rather than always in 'teaching';
- their function as observers and assessors of children's understandings as well as outcomes;
- their obligation clearly to conceptualize the whole curriculum of which the National Curriculum is a part.

When we consider the *context* of pedagogy, this focus subsumes such aspects as the learning environment, school ethos and the actual classroom and school. It also includes such elements as:

- the physical environment – indoors and outdoors;
- the social environment of school and schooling (e.g. is the child an outcome of the context or has the context influenced the child?);
- the psychological environment of school and schooling;
- the philosophical considerations within schools and aspects such as teacher's beliefs and values;
- the curriculum context, including the National Curriculum where this is relevant and appropriate, but also showing where this does not necessarily meet pedagogical needs;
- the frameworks within which the whole concept of schooling takes place and where this fits education in a broader sense.

The overall rationale for each book in the series starts from a belief that teachers should be enabled to analyse their own practices in specific aspects of the broader curriculum as a major aspect of their professionalism. The books are particularly useful at a time of continual curriculum fluctuation when reflection is being focused back upon the child and pedagogy generally as the only perpetuating and consistent elements.

As an integral component, all the books weave teachers' assessment of children's learning and understanding into each particular focus, the intention being to show how the planning>learning> assessment>planning cycle is vital to the quality and success of children's and teachers' learning experiences. With practical ideas, challenges and direct relationships to classroom practice, these books offer ways of establishing theory as *the* adjunct to practice through teachers' thinking about how they already operate such approaches in the classroom, and how they may enrich, extend and advance their practices to the mutual benefit of themselves, the children, the curriculum and education in society as a whole.

Successful children, successful teaching has its foundation in sound and up-to-date psychological theory and is written in a clear, very accessible (and inimitable!) style by Roger Merry. As an educational psychologist who has worked in primary initial teacher education for several years, Roger has recognized that, despite the valuable and informative work done by psychologists into pedagogy, there has consistently been a recurring gap between their work in carrying out studies under controlled conditions, and the everyday work of teachers in classrooms. Furthermore, as public demands on teachers have increased, psychologists have given greater focus to exploring learning in 'real' settings and increasingly recognized the importance and complexity of the intermix of children's attitudes, teachers' professional understanding and classroom contexts.

In a characteristically engaging and humorous way, Roger takes a broad view of the concept of 'competence', pointing out that this is not simply related to teaching and learning behaviours but to what the learner already knows and can, therefore, already bring to bear on the learning context and content. Competence, it follows, must include social and emotional competences as well as specifically cognitive ones and, equally, cannot be divorced from cultural and attitudinal aspects.

The cameos presented offer many examples of life in general, and classroom life in particular, with which primary teachers will definitely empathize. In themselves, and taking another main focus of the book, the cameos are carefully considered observations of pedagogical issues and insights in educational contexts. Readers will quickly recognize Roger's commitment to engaging children in their own learning processes and outcomes as a major way of both assessing and understanding their learning needs and understanding the implications for the teacher's role.

This book offers a significant contribution to our understanding of the ways in which recent ideas from psychology can be adopted by busy primary teachers to enrich the curriculum provision they make for young learners as well as assisting them in fulfilling external and school demands. Even the titles of the chapters will inevitably tease and challenge teachers to think about practice in decidedly different ways.

So settle down for an enjoyable, stimulating and thought-provoking professional 'read' as you enter the world of 'Vimto with Beryl'!

Janet Moyles

Acknowledgements

There are a number of people who have supported the development of this book. First of all I would like to acknowledge the series editor, Janet Moyles, who has encouraged, nudged and generally guided the project along and who has also supplied some of the photographs, illustrations and layout advice. Aliya Ahmed has also been a great help in aspects of typing and Cherry Fulloway was kind enough to offer some further photographs to support the text.

To anyone who recognizes themselves in the text and who has clearly, inadvertently as well as overtly, fed my thinking, I am delighted to have known you and people like you!

I am greatly indebted to Deb and the boys for their patience and tolerance (if not always wild enthusiasm!) in supporting me in successfully completing this manuscript.

Introduction: Vimto with Beryl

Let me begin by telling you something you can't possibly already know about.

Cameo

When I was 9 years old and in the class of the formidable 'Maggie' Mercer at King Street Primary school, there was one girl who was undoubtedly the centre of attraction for all us boys. Her name was Susan; she had blonde curly hair, she was disturbingly pretty, and she knew it. Being low in the male pecking order, I knew my place and had to be content with admiring her from afar, being particularly careful not to upset Barry Woods, the undisputed 'cock' of the class, who naturally saw her as his own.

But I gradually became increasingly aware of another girl in the class. She was dark and quiet and mysterious, and her name was Beryl. My parents encouraged me to invite friends for tea, and I eventually plucked up courage to ask Beryl, praying that they wouldn't tease me. It was a bit awkward at first because she seemed strangely uninterested in my stamp collection, or even in kicking a tennis ball against the wall, but we were saved by the comfortable ritual of tea-time – tinned fruit salad (one cherry each), condensed milk and bread and butter. Much to my relief, we spent most of the meal exactly as I did with boys who came for tea, in uncontrollable fits of the giggles, which my parents treated as always with amused tolerance. It wasn't exactly cider with Rosie but it was certainly Vimto with Beryl.

> Two days later Alistair Carter bought her some chocolates. Real chocolates in a proper box. She never spoke to me again.

Having read this far, you already will have learned a little about something you did not know before (unless you are Beryl, of course, in which case I'd love to hear from you . . .). In a sense, I can therefore claim to have taught you something, no matter how trivial or self-indulgent. But how could we decide how successful the teaching and learning have been?

One obvious and well-tried way would be to ask questions. So, pencils out, name, date and margin, and number down one to four!

1 What was the name of the school?
2 What was Beryl's surname?
3 What was the name of the class bully?
4 Why did we two children get on better during tea?

Though the story and questions are trivial, they raise a lot of issues about the nature of successful teaching and learning, which in turn will reappear as major themes in this book. For instance, the first question could be easily answered just by copying a few words from the text, so the teaching and learning have both been successful. Of course, it could be argued that such a trivial activity does not represent real teaching or learning, but it does reflect day-to-day practice in many classrooms.

Question two may have been slightly irritating because it broke the rules. It was impossible to answer, even though it was equally straightforward and factual, because the necessary information was not in the passage. If I had intended you to know her full name, I didn't 'teach' you appropriately and the failure is mine as a teacher rather than yours as a learner. We will return to this important point in a moment, after a brief discussion of the other questions.

Question three is not as easy as it looks. The word 'bully' is not in the passage and it could again be argued that the required information was not there. However, there is an important difference. Beryl's surname is arbitrary – it cannot be deduced from the available information – but the name of the bully can be inferred, not simply from the passage, but by combining the text with the reader's prior knowledge. Even if a reader did not know the exact meaning of the word 'cock' in 1950s children's slang, they could infer what it meant from the rest of the passage because they understood the writer's nervousness at the thought of upsetting Barry. However, if the reader really did understand the slang term, they might argue that the 'cock' of the class was simply the toughest boy and, like Barry, not necessarily a bully at all. In fact, like a teacher with good control, Barry was so self-assured about his position that he rarely needed to demonstrate his authority and left any menial bashing to his henchmen, who were thus the real bullies.

So even this apparently simple question raises several important issues about the nature of successful learning. Learners often do not have all the necessary facts presented to them and need to recognize this to decide if they can supplement the given information by what they already know. Nor is such prior knowledge purely 'cognitive' in the sense of being straightforward information, since it often involves understanding individuals' feelings and social situations: in this case the inference is possible only if the reader appreciates the writer's feelings of anxiety about annoying Barry and the quite complex social roles of the pecking-order. These social and emotional factors may operate in more subtle ways too: some readers might feel slightly irritated by question two because an unspoken rule between reader and writer is being broken – that the writer must not ask the reader unanswerable 'comprehension' questions.

These social and emotional factors were much more apparent in the final 'why' question. Not everybody would be aware of the subtle nuances and cultural conventions of a Lancashire tea-time, such as the crucial distribution of the tinned cherries, but most would be able to understand the idea of 'the comfortable ritual' of the meal and see how it made things easier, because of their own awareness of conventions and feelings.

Learners can thus make powerful inferences which enable them to go well beyond presented information, not only through their cognitive skills and knowledge, but also through their awareness of feelings and cultural behaviour. In terms of subject content, the relative importance of these varies, of course. Attitudes and social awareness may seem irrelevant when teaching about insulation, for example, though teachers in Iceland and Bali would probably approach it quite differently. The importance attached to a topic depends a great deal on cultural values, as becomes even more apparent if a lesson on insulation includes conservation issues or anything else that involves people. More importantly, even if culture and attitudes do not seem directly related to the actual material, school learning itself takes place in particular social settings, the curriculum is defined by the values of the culture, and children's feelings and attitudes are crucial to their success or failure as learners.

This introduction has shown that, even in the case of an apparently trivial story and a few straightforward questions about it, there are complex factors involved in successful teaching and learning. Psychologists have discovered a great deal about these factors, and would seem to have a lot to offer to teachers, yet in the past, their work does appear to have had little immediate direct impact on what actually goes on in schools.

Certainly, it is tempting from the safety of my word processor to ignore this apparent lack of impact of psychology and simply to outline some of its ideas before piously concluding that 'teachers should be aware' of them. But if we are to take the ideas seriously, we do need to consider why there often seems to be a gap between the findings of psychologists and the practices of teachers. There are three possible points to consider, and they relate closely to the structure of this book and the others in the series, as outlined in Janet Moyles' preface:

- Psychologists work to a different agenda from teachers, with different methods and priorities, so that much of the research on children's learning is inaccessible to classroom practitioners (Newman *et al.* 1989). Some major theories, such as those of Piaget, do have an enormous influence eventually, but it may take years for them to filter through to teachers in ways that are useful and applicable, and they may even become distorted on the way. The sections on the *child* in each chapter of this book have been written mainly to try to respond to this, by summarizing and discussing some important ideas about how children learn, in ways that are relevant for teachers.
- Another explanation is that we normally take our own cognitive processes, attitudes and social settings for granted. Teachers given a few blessed minutes to spare at breaktime do not pause to do a bit of perceiving, or to try out a new emotion, or to reflect on the social context of the staffroom! Yet we can surely learn a great deal about how the human mind works

by stopping to consider our own thoughts and feelings. Another intention of this book is to encourage such reflection, particularly in the sections which focus on *teachers* and their own thinking.

- A third explanation is that it is quite possible for adults to be aware, and even approve, of such ideas without being willing to apply them to their own learning or teaching (Sotto 1994). Richardson (1992) notes wryly that even lecturers in cognitive psychology make little use of its ideas in their own teaching! The chapter sections on the *context* of teaching and learning are an attempt to show how ideas derived from the findings of psychologists can be realistically applied to the work of teachers.

The introductory cameo suggests that we can usefully consider four sorts of factors which affect successful learning and teaching:

- factors which can be observed and assessed, such as the correct few words of text to copy out in answer to the first question about the name of the school;
- cognitive processes such as making inferences to work out the answer to the third question about the name of the bully;
- underlying attitudes and feelings which may encourage or inhibit learning – for example enabling us to empathize with the writer and answer the question about why the children got on better during tea;
- social factors which underpin all forms of communication, including writing, and which therefore affect all situations in which learning occurs.

Each of these four general factors is the focus of a chapter in the book. Chapter 1 considers how far it is possible to define and improve classroom success by concentrating on observable behaviour in both teachers and learners. It will become clear that such an emphasis is helpful only up to a point, and the chapter ends by introducing the other three factors. Chapter 2 examines the cognitive processes which are central to successful learning, while Chapter 3 looks at how these processes develop in children. Chapter 4 considers the feelings and attitudes which have already been shown as crucial for success, and Chapter 5 discusses the particular social contexts in which school learning takes place.

We now turn to an approach to successful teaching and learning which seems to hold considerable promise and which has increasingly found favour with many of those in charge of the education system in this country – the notion of competence.

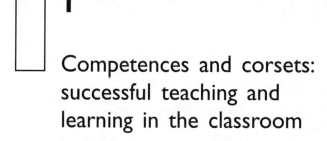

I

Competences and corsets: successful teaching and learning in the classroom

Introduction: educational competences – the behavioural background

As we have seen in the introductory cameo about drinking Vimto with Beryl, the first question at least seemed straightforward and it was very easy to say what was wrong with the second question. Is it possible to make real-life classroom teaching and learning more like this, so that we could be clear not only about what is to be learned but also about how we can check on our children's learning and on our own success as teachers?

Some would argue that it is not only possible but crucial, and could refer to a considerable amount of psychological research to support their argument. Such a point of view could be traced back to a long tradition of 'behavioural' psychology, though the term may conjure up images of salivating dogs and lever-pressing rats. If you want to know more, the background to behaviourism is presented in most introductory psychology texts, such as Myers (1995), or in general educational psychology books such as Desforges (1995).

Very briefly, behaviourists say that we can never directly study thinking, feelings or anything that goes on 'inside the head', but can only make inferences about them from behaviour, so that psychologists should concentrate only on what they can observe. This is certainly a powerful argument and one which dominated Western psychology for many years and indirectly gave rise to some influential ideas about how to improve children's learning in school. At risk of grossly over-simplifying such approaches, they tend to have five basic steps:

- establish a 'baseline' of what the child can already do, expressed as tightly as possible in terms of their behaviour;
- establish a set of goals, similarly tightly expressed in terms of desired behaviour, setting priorities and short-term objectives as appropriate;
- look at the baseline and the objectives, and break down the differences into very small steps to set up a programme;
- work through the programme, minimizing errors and providing lots of feedback and positive reinforcement;
- monitor the child's progress and review the programme as appropriate.

In some cases, the child may work through an established programme which cannot be modified and where their baseline and progress are assessed by tests built into the programme itself, and programmes can be set up to improve behaviour as well as learning. (For more discussion of behavioural approaches, see Wheldall *et al.* 1986, and for actual examples in practice, see Merrett 1993.)

Against this background, one set of approaches, loosely grouped under the general heading of the 'competence' movement, has become very influential, apparently offering a way of making both children's learning and teachers' performance more open, more able to be monitored, and thus ultimately more successful. At first sight, the rationale behind behavioural competences certainly sounds reasonable and convincing, and we can find out a great deal about children's skills by observing their behaviour. To be able to prove that a child has learned something, the teacher needs to be able to say what the evidence will be that learning has taken place, and such evidence needs to be expressed in clear, observable terms describing exactly what the child will do. For instance, a behavioural objective might be that children should be able to 'add correctly pairs of single digits under ten'. Yet, far from being grateful for such clarity, many of those who have the most experience of competence statements are often the most critical. Hyland (1994: x) for instance, describes competence-based education in no uncertain terms as 'logically and conceptually

We can find out a great deal about children's skills by observing their behaviour

confused, epistemologically ambiguous and based on largely discredited behaviourist learning principles'. If we are to pursue the notions of the successful child and the successful teacher any further, we need to look more carefully at these and other criticisms.

In keeping with the format of the following chapters and other books in the series, the rest of this chapter is organized for convenience into three overlapping sections, emphasizing respectively children's learning, the role of the teacher, and the contexts in which teaching and learning take place.

Behavioural competences and children's learning

Practical problems

Because they seem relatively straightforward to describe, basic literacy and numeracy skills are frequently chosen to illustrate examples of competence statements. For example, it is clearly important for children to be able to add and subtract small numbers, and expressing this as an objective that children should, for example, 'know addition and subtraction facts up to 20' seems a reasonable statement of competence. However, one problem arises immediately because adding a verb like 'know' to a phrase describing some part of the curriculum does not necessarily produce something which can be measured or tested. What exactly does it mean to 'know' something? Such questions have kept philosophers in business for centuries, but this is not just a philosophical problem, because even an apparently innocuous sentence like this raises far more practical questions than it answers. For example:

- What sort of aid is the child allowed to use? Fingers? Cubes? A calculator? None?
- How quickly do they have to answer? Immediately? Or is it more important that they can work out the answer if necessary?
- Are the sums presented only orally (in which case what does a deaf child do?) or written down, so that children have to know the symbols? If the latter, in what format? (e.g. '3 + ? = 9' or 'What do you get if you add three and six?')
- Similarly, is the child required to write the answer down? If so, and if for example they reverse one of the symbols, does that matter?
- Can the sums be embedded in problems about sweets etc.?

Anyone who has taught young children will recognize that these are not trivial questions – children may seem perfectly competent at adding pairs of digits until they are prevented from using their fingers, have to give an instant response, deal with a different format of the question or solve it when it is embedded in a 'real' problem. Nor are these simply difficulties which can be solved by a series of arbitrary decisions about practical arrangements, because they raise real questions about the very nature of learning competence. Unfortunately, (or perhaps fortunately) the solution does not seem to lie in specifying even more detailed, childproof objectives, because there are more deep-seated objections to applying behavioural competences wholeheartedly to children's learning.

Problems of definition

Some writers (e.g. Norris 1991) have objected to the use of the term 'competence' because, although it sounds like something everybody wants, there is conceptual confusion and a lack of any commonly-agreed definition about what the word means. Others have tried to tighten up the definitions – Hyland (1995) proposes an interesting distinction between 'competence' as a general capacity more properly applied to people and 'competency' as being more applicable to particular tasks. Certainly, clarity would be welcome, especially about an approach which itself claims to be bringing a tighter, much needed objectivity to teaching and learning. But, to be fair, there are many other words which we happily use, both within education and outside, which also lack full agreement on a tight definition. Indeed, it sometimes seems that the more important a word is, the less agreement there will be about exactly what it means! We can define what a 'full stop' is (though even here there is room for occasional disagreement about its use) but controversies about exactly what we mean by 'reading' or 'adolescence' have kept academics busy for years, while the fact that even the European Community would not attempt to establish a legal definition of the word 'love' has thankfully not stopped it being a major human preoccupation.

Problems with some areas of learning

A more fundamental objection is that, among all the things children have to learn, there are many that are not going to be turned easily into statements of behavioural competence. Thus the 1995 National Curriculum Attainment Target 2 for Art Key Stage 1 was that 'Pupils describe and compare images and artefacts in simple terms. They recognize differences in methods and approaches used and make links with their own art, craft and design work'.

As aims, these are highly commendable, and few teachers would argue with them or want to make them more prescriptive, but they are far too 'fuzzy' to be statements of behavioural competences. However, any attempt to change the above general aims into objective behavioural statements will be defeated by the very personal nature of what we are trying to describe. It would be possible, of course, to set up competence statements only for those areas where it is easier to do so, but there would be a danger of creating some sort of two-tier curriculum emphasizing some areas of learning, not because they were more important, but simply because it was easier to write competence statements for them.

It seems, then, that there are some important areas of children's learning in school that would be very difficult to reduce to competence statements. But there are even deeper objections involving our notions of all human learning.

Problems with the nature of all learning

In seeking to reduce learning to what can be specified objectively, behavioural competences run the risk of ignoring those very aspects of human learning which make it so worthwhile and important. For example, a competent performance may be conscious or unconscious, but an emphasis solely on what the performer can *do* ignores what they may or may not *understand* about their performance. An extreme example would be those once referred to as 'idiots savants' who can, for example, immediately name the day of the week on which any given date (such as 21 February 1945) fell, but who do not seem to understand basic mathematical processes such as dividing by seven. (To be fair, of course, it is possible to make inferences about their understanding only from their behaviour.) This is not a trivial or purely 'philosophical' point since, as we shall see, the level of awareness can have major effects on vital practical issues such as whether or not the learner can transfer that skill to other settings, or teach someone else to perform it. Similarly, an emphasis on observable behaviour ignores the feelings, attitudes and intentions of the learner, and these factors are not inconvenient side-effects but are crucial to successful learning.

Moreover, if 'real' learning involves a relationship between teacher and learner and relies on what both of them bring to the learning experience, then it becomes very difficult to specify in advance exactly what learning will take place. As Bonnett (1994) puts it:

Precisely what it is to be a learner, what it is to be a teacher, are not separately pre-specifiable, but emerge from the particular situations created by a set of reciprocal relationships. This is clearly at odds with those current approaches to curriculum planning which increasingly demand that all such things are carefully defined in advance. Clarity of purpose is therefore conflated with pre-set standards and goals, which run across and obscure the demands of real learning.

(Bonnet 1994: 179)

In sum, behavioural competences do appear very attractive and do seem to offer a way to structure and chart children's learning, but the very attractions that they offer may also imply a restricted view of what learning is really about. Moreover, it will be immediately apparent that many of the points made already will apply not only to *learning* but also, directly or indirectly, to *teaching*.

Competences and teaching

Teacher competences – restricted or vague?

The National Curriculum was seen by many as a step towards a more objective and standardized approach to children's learning, and the government was equally keen to produce actual lists of competences expected of newly-qualified teachers. Yet a glance at such lists shows immediately that many of them ran into problems. Thus Thompson (1992) notes that

. . . some competences seem – like the belief that performance-related pay is a pre-eminent motivator – to come from the Pavlovian behaviourist view of human nature: 'to devise and use appropriate rewards and sanctions to maintain an effective learning environment'. Others are so ill-defined, such as 'a readiness to promote the moral and spiritual well-being of pupils', that it is difficult to know what responsibilities you might be letting yourself in for as a teacher . . .

(Thompson 1992: 4)

One response to this problem has been to recognize the limitations of pure behavioural competences and to write competence statements which involve cognitive skills such as being aware of safety aspects of situations or being able to identify and reflect on experiences. Kitson (1995) discusses such examples, showing how they do not simply present 'bits' of behaviour to be checked on a list, but encourage teachers to reflect on their own performance. Similarly, when the Teacher Training Agency (TTA) began to develop competences for newly-qualified teachers, they recognized that highly specific behavioural competences would be impractical and instead proposed five 'areas of competence':

- knowledge and understanding of the curriculum;
- subject knowledge and subject application;
- teaching strategies and techniques, and class management;
- assessment and recording of pupil progress;
- foundation for further professional development.

(TTA 1994: 4)

Even here, a glance at the actual statements reveals their behavioural roots in that they all begin with a verb like 'identify', 'present' or 'use' which suggests that the desired behaviour can be objectively observed, but the statements are usually, in fact, general to the point of vagueness. For instance, primary teachers should 'demonstrate understanding of the purposes, scope, structure and balance of the primary curriculum as a whole' or should 'develop effective working relationships with colleagues and parents'.

Perhaps in recognition of this vagueness, the TTA later proposed to replace these general competences with pages of specific 'standards' to be required of newly-qualified teachers. For example: 'Those to be awarded Qualified Teacher status should, when assessed, demonstrate that they ... set a good example to the children they teach, through their presentation and their personal and professional conduct' (TTA 1997: 11).

Such statements are as unobjectionable as apple pie or motherhood, but it is misleading to imply that, because they are expressed as 'competences' – as things teachers should actually do – they offer much practical help, and most would be equally at home among the pious clichés of the average 'mission statement'.

The root of the dilemma for competence statements is that, if they limit themselves to observable behaviour, they need to be very cumbersome while still ignoring vital aspects of teaching, yet the alternative is to be so woolly that they are useless as

statements of measurable behaviour. Thus the TTA areas of competence recognize the complexities of teaching, but offer little
practical help. Conversely, behavioural competence statements
run the risk of ignoring not only the complexities of learning, but
also the equally complex and problematic nature of teaching,
with its need for critical reflection and professional judgement
(Hustler and McIntyre 1996). At the extremes, statements could
either force teachers to become simply mechanistic deliverers of
tightly-scripted materials, as they seem to be in some countries,
or offer so little practical guidance as to be almost worthless.

Competences and power

In spite of such dilemmas, competence statements do have
attractions. For overloaded teachers, workable statements enabling objective assessment and monitoring of children's learning
would seem a boon. They are similarly attractive to those who
evaluate teachers so that competences are clearly very compatible with an assessment-driven educational system. If it is possible
to produce useful statements, they make the aims and content of
what is to be learned clear and open for all to see, rather than
keeping them as the 'secret' preserve of the teacher. Similarly,
children are encouraged to identify their own strengths and needs,
making them active participants in their own learning, so that
the competence movement could be seen as democratic and
empowering from the learner's point of view (Kitson 1995).

Yet it is possible to argue precisely the opposite, noting that
individual strengths and needs can be identified, but only in
terms of the programme, and that the programme itself is not usually modifiable to meet those individual needs. Viewed in this
light, what competences offer is not democracy but control. Thus
Sotto (1994) regards the movement as extremely authoritarian
rather than democratic because the statements of competence are
essentially 'givens', which simply have to be accepted passively
by both teachers and learners.

Hyland (1995) notes that competence-based instruction is in
danger of serving the needs of bureaucrats rather than students.
In fact, the competence movement is very much in line with general trends in education such as government control of the curriculum and increased public accountability. It also fits in with
more instrumental views of the nature of learning itself, in which

content is 'delivered' like so much milk, under the watchful eyes and clipboards of those in charge of 'quality control', and where the children are seen merely as the classic 'empty vessels' (presumably cereal bowls in this case!). Perhaps that is its great attraction as well as its major flaw.

Beyond the competent teacher

So far, it has been demonstrated that the behavioural roots of the competence movement, while apparently offering a way of making successful teaching and learning more open and objective, also imply a restricted view of what teaching and learning are all about. Part of the problem lies with the everyday use of the word 'competent'. Of course, if somebody is asked whether or not they want the teachers of their children to be competent, they will reply that they do, just as they would prefer teachers also to be sane and sober. Equally, however, if they are told that their child's teacher is 'quite competent', they will be waiting for the word 'but' to appear next. 'Competent' is one of those words like 'average' or 'adequate' which can appear simply to damn with faint praise.

So what should actually be expected of a competent teacher? Amongst other things, they would presumably have adequate knowledge of their subject, satisfactory class control and reliable record-keeping, and all these appeared in the 1994 TTA lists. Yet, while these things are undeniably important, do they really capture the qualities of a successful teacher – the one that parents secretly hope will be allocated to their child's class next year?

The Times Educational Supplement series in which famous people describe 'my best teacher' gives us one insight into what a wide range of individuals might really want teachers to be like. They are fascinating, funny, often touching accounts, recognizing the debt that the writers owe, and serving as reminders of the enormous effects teachers can have, sometimes even through a chance remark or something they were hardly aware of at the time. And what sort of teachers do these articles talk about? What they do *not* describe are 'competent' teachers with adequate subject knowledge, satisfactory class control and reliable record-keeping. Mark Tully, the BBC correspondent and journalist, gave an account which is in many ways typical. His 'best teacher':

... had a lovely chuckle and smiling eyes, and a tremendous sense of humour. He was very anti-establishment. A naughty man in many ways, a delightful man ... We had a very unorthodox education under him ... He was very charismatic and good. He woke my interest in reading and learning.

(Tully 1996. 24)

The actress Patricia Hodge went even further in describing her 'best teacher':

She had great presence and could be quite outrageous ... for instance, to help us learn about tens and units, she would work sums on the board and every time we had to 'carry one' she would proclaim 'Change!' in ringing tones and lift up her jumper to show her pink silk corsets. It was something you never forgot.

(Hodge 1995: 20)

In fact, what comes through time and time again are fond memories of teachers with flair, warmth and humour; these were teachers whose own enthusiasm for learning inspired their pupils. They were often charismatic, even eccentric – the very last people whose qualities could be pinned down by a series of standardized behavioural competences.

There is a need for care here, however. One of the reasons behind the memorable success of these teachers might be that they were not the same as most of the rest, and an entire staff composed of such people would probably be not only a Head's nightmare, but also an educational disaster area. The writers are also looking back with a certain amount of nostalgia and are themselves successful (and possibly charismatic) people who were able to enjoy and benefit from being taught by such characters. We need to resist the temptation to set up some sort of false dichotomy, with an idealized, romantic view of 'good teachers' as charismatic eccentrics with a great sense of humour on the one hand, and 'bad teachers' as dull conformists with neat registers on the other. Such a view would not only be unhelpful to teachers who have to work in the real world of the National Curriculum and Ofsted inspections, but would also present a false idea of what teaching and learning are really about. It is certainly not a view which is being advocated here: there is more to teaching than flashing pink corsets!

What *is* being said here is that there is also more to teaching than can be expressed in terms of behavioural competences, and that some of the most important qualities and skills of successful teachers are precisely those which are the most difficult to describe in such terms. In fact, they may be difficult to assess objectively at all: one shudders at the thought of Ofsted inspectors rating a teacher as 'sound' in unorthodoxy or 'weak' in charisma.

So what more do we want?

Competences in context

In spite of their attractions, behavioural competences are limited in value and need to be considered in the context of other underlying factors which are vital in promoting successful teaching and learning. Statements about behaviour describe only observable products or outcomes, but the invisible processes going on 'inside the heads' of children and teachers are at least as important, even if we can ultimately only make inferences about them from the behaviour we observe. As the introduction showed, coupled with these *cognitive* aspects are sets of *attitudes* and *emotions* which have crucial effects on the success of teachers or learners. Children and teachers also operate within *social contexts* which also strongly affect what can be taught or learned. These three important factors – *cognitive*, *emotional*, and *social*, form the basis for the following chapters, and are only briefly introduced in what follows.

Think back to the quotation from Patricia Hodge about her 'best teacher', but don't actually look back at it. What were the first two words in the first sentence quoted? No peeping!

Too difficult? A clue would be that the first two words were either 'bacon sandwich', 'the and' or 'she had'. Which phrase was it?

Easier? Let's consider what would appear to be a much harder question, asking about far more than two words, without any clues at all: what did this teacher do in order to remind her class to 'carry one' when doing sums on the board? To get the most out of this activity, it would be useful to write the answer down on a bit of paper.

Though admittedly trivial, these three questions in fact reveal a great deal about cognitive processes such as attention, perception and memory which are clearly at the heart of successful learning, but which teachers rarely have the time to stop to think about. For a start, let's think exactly why the first question was so difficult, looking for explanations in terms of memory, perception and attention.

Memory

It could be that every single word we read is stored in our memories, in which case the problem would be that the answer is there somewhere but we are not always able to retrieve it. Some psychologists do think that we can store enormous amounts of information and that the bottleneck is at the stage of retrieval rather than storage, either because of interference from other things we have learned, or even because we sometimes actually want to forget or alter our memories of unpleasant things. This is a well-established area of psychological research, but not the sort of explanation most people would consider the most likely in this case. (For a detailed discussion of the nature of memory and its implications for teachers, see Stevick 1996.)

Perception

It could be that some people would fail to answer the first question because they simply didn't understand it, or didn't understand the original passage: in other words, they were not able to perceive them properly. This would be a valid explanation in the case of a poor reader who could slowly identify most of the individual words but could retain little of the overall meaning – a situation familiar to many teachers. Perception and memory are very strongly linked together in a variety of ways, as we shall see later, and even common sense would suggest that if a learner doesn't understand something in the first place, it will be very difficult to remember.

Attention

A third possible explanation is to do with attention – that, although the opening words were understandable in context at the time of reading, they were not given particular attention, so that they never got stored in any sort of lasting or retrievable way. Most people would regard this as the most likely sort of explanation.

Turning to question two, what made this so much easier, and what does it show about human learning?

Using clues: the case of the bacon sandwich

Logically, or if the human mind functioned like a computer, it would seem that the three clues should not help, since the words were impossible to recall and were therefore not available to be compared with the three possible answers given. In practice, of course, recognition is generally much easier than recall because we do not have to start from scratch and are able to sift through a few alternatives to decide which looks the best. In situations like this, we don't really remember the words at all, but simply make an intelligent guess.

So exactly how did the clues help, and how was it possible to decide so confidently? The first possibility, 'bacon sandwich' was extremely unlikely because of the subject of the passage, so it could be rejected on the grounds of meaning. The second possibility was equally unlikely, but for a different reason: even though the two words 'the' and 'and' are very common and could both easily have occurred in the passage, they simply do not occur together in this order. Here, you used not your understanding of the particular content or meaning of the passage, but your general knowledge of how the English language is structured. In both cases, you did not rely on some sort of stored memory of the passage, but on what you already knew, in the first case semantic knowledge, and in the second syntactic knowledge.

Getting the gist

Even though the third question asked for a lot more than a couple of words to be remembered, with no clues, it is easier than the first question. The actual answer, quoted from the passage, is that 'she would proclaim "Change!" in ringing tones and lift up her jumper to show her pink silk corsets'. If you did write down your answer, it will not be exactly the same as the original, because when you first read the passage, you were focusing your attention on the meaning rather than the exact words, and in any case you would not interpret the question as calling for the exact words of the original. Instead, you remembered the gist or general idea: you probably recalled that she showed her corsets, but maybe not that she shouted 'Change!' and you almost certainly used simpler words of your own rather than 'proclaimed' or 'in ringing tones'.

Although teachers do sometimes expect children to recall pieces of information exactly 'word for word' (such as multiplication tables), most of the time we want them to understand and remember general ideas. When we get them to write down even very 'factual' information for topics, for example, we usually dislike them copying the exact words of the source material and encourage them to use their own words, to show that they have understood.

How do we do it?

In fact, psychologists still have a lot to find out about how memory works, and it is interesting to consider the sorts of things learners do when faced with complex material like a text. For instance, many people form visual images of what they read, and are therefore able to reconstruct the meaning of a passage at least partly from the visual image. Such strategies are very important in successful learning, and we will consider them in more detail in Chapter 3.

It is also interesting to think about why some things are more memorable than others. If you did remember the bit about the corsets (and I promise not to mention them again after this!) why was it? Was it because the whole idea is so unusual, comic or bizarre? Certainly, such bizarre images have been recommended by memory experts since the time of the ancient Greeks (Yates 1966) and they do seem to grab our attention – which is probably why the teacher did it in the first place.

Metacognition

The three questions also reveal something about some of the higher order processes of learning which take many years to develop and which are also discussed further in Chapter 3. To a successful learner, the first question can be immediately recognized as impossibly difficult and dismissed as such, with no attempt to answer. This is not a trivial point, and one skill that successful learners have to develop is knowing when a task or problem is not worth tackling because the effort is not worth the result (Claxton 1996).

The second question does not appear so ridiculous, even to someone who already knew that they could not remember the two words. Instead, most adults would look at the question, realize that they had a fighting chance and so consider the three alternatives. If so, they would be able to guess that the correct answer was 'she had' and, if asked, would feel quite confident about it.

Similarly, the third question is interpreted as asking for the general meaning rather than the exact words because to ask for verbatim recall would again be ridiculously demanding, and a waste of time to attempt. In all three cases, the questions required an awareness of thinking processes themselves, deciding for example what each question required and how easy it would be to answer. Such awareness of our own thinking is called 'metacognition' and it has recently become an area of particular interest to many psychologists.

To the extent that a successful teacher must be a 'reflective practitioner' rather than a mere delivery service, teaching too requires complex metacognitive skills. A sensitive teacher can predict and recognize the cognitive difficulties that children experience, and can think about how to present information in ways that are likely to maximize learning. Thus Jordan and Powell (1995: 120), in their discussion of competence-based models of teacher education, note that 'acquisition of skills does not relate directly to competency. To be competent is both to have sets of skills *and* be able to employ them, using a flexible, responsive set of higher-order strategies'.

Such issues will be taken up in more detail in the next chapter, but for a discussion of cognitive limitations and some of their implications for teachers, see Merry (1995).

Attitudes, teaching and learning

The three questions about Patricia Hodges' 'best teacher' involve more than a range of cognitive skills in isolation. Although the exercise was hardly likely to raise strong emotions, the impossibly difficult first question may appear slightly irritating, and we must certainly be careful not to isolate cognitive skills from feelings and attitudes when we consider children's learning.

In traditional psychology textbooks, there were usually separate chapters with titles like 'perception', 'memory' and 'attitudes' and while these terms offer a convenient way of organizing discussion of complex processes, it has become increasingly apparent that they are inextricably bound up with each other in reality. If we accept that learning is not a passive taking-in of what is delivered, but is a highly active process which depends a great deal on the learner, then we must also recognize that the attitudes of learners are not an optional side-issue which may be vaguely affected by learning success or failure, but are very much involved in causing that success or failure in the first place. Successful and unsuccessful learners have very different attitudes, not only towards problems, but also towards themselves as learners, and again, part of a good teacher's job will obviously be to foster positive attitudes.

Unfortunately for the writers of behavioural competences, attitudes and emotions are even harder than cognitive skills to express in behavioural terms. However, from the teacher's point of view, it is still worth considering how children might express their attitudes. Mager (1990), for example, discusses what he calls SMATS (Subject Matter Approach Tendencies) and SMUTS (Subject Matter Unapproach Tendencies). While such acronyms may themselves raise SMUTS in some readers, it is none the less worth asking what sort of evidence we tend to use as teachers to decide whether or not children feel positive about themselves and their work. Groans of dismay when the next activity is announced, attempts to pack up ten minutes early or classic work-avoidance strategies like obsessive pencil sharpening will tell an experienced teacher a lot about children's attitudes.

However, an emphasis on positive attitudes is not meant to imply that children should be cocooned in classrooms with rose-tinted windows and never be faced with difficulties which might challenge their happy frames of mind. Significantly, one of the mainstays of a strict behavioural approach to learning was that it should proceed in very small steps and should, as far as possible, be 'error-free' so that children should not have the opportunity to practise incorrect responses in case they learned these instead of the correct ones. Although logical, and sometimes effective for children with learning difficulties, behaviourally-based materials like those produced for 'programmed instruction' books and machines ran the risk of becoming tedious and of not fostering positive attitudes so much as causing an actual decline in motivation through terminal boredom. In contrast, most views of learning which emphasize cognitive processes imply just the opposite – that children in fact have to recognize discrepancies and mistakes in their assumptions in order for learning to take place at all. Claxton (1984: 145) thus says that successful learners are comfortable with failure, and actually defines learning as 'what happens when you take the risk of not being competent'.

Teachers' own attitudes are equally crucial. As teachers, we can act as models for how to cope with failure or disappointment, and we quickly realize how important it is to encourage children's learning by appearing confident and enthusiastic ourselves, even if we actually feel nervous or jaded. In both teaching and learning, cognitive and emotional factors therefore affect each other in complex ways, and these will be explored more fully in Chapter 4.

Social factors, teaching and learning

Until quite recently, social psychology was considered to be rather separate from other branches of psychology, to the extent that some universities offered it as a distinct subject. There are also several related areas of study such as anthropology and sociology where research has tended to have little direct impact on the work of psychologists interested in children's learning. More recently, however, the degree of overlapping interest has been recognized, and areas of study such as 'social cognition' have become more popular. Like attitudes and emotions, the social context of learning is increasingly recognized as more than a side-issue or incidental background, and we are coming to understand how the experiences of individuals interact with the cultures in which they live, often in subtle and complex ways. (See Bruner 1996; Bennett 1993 or Resnick and Collins 1994.)

The concept of competence illustrates this well because it involves skills and understanding which are essentially socially defined. For instance, we expect taxi drivers not only to know their way around, but also to be able to drive while delivering a

monologue over their left shoulder. A London cab driver therefore needs not only to have the motor skills (if you'll pardon the
pun) to pass the driving test but also has to acquire 'The Knowledge' of London's streets. The skills and knowledge involved
have been publicly agreed, and we have a right to expect our
driver to be competent in these respects without having to check
nervously every time we get into a taxi. Similarly, the notion of
what constitutes a competent teacher clearly depends on the
values of the particular culture and the role expectations it has
about teachers.

However, it does seem that such explicit, socially agreed competences do not tell the whole story when we try to apply them to
more complex roles involving professional attitudes or personal
relationships. As we have seen, statements of competence can
describe only observable behaviour, such as the ability to get
into third gear or find the most expensive route to Mornington
Crescent, but they are also limited to those aspects of a role which
can be publicly agreed – they cannot really deal with the personalities, attitudes or needs of individuals. Certainly, it would be a
brave person who would even attempt to define the delicate interpersonal skills or political views which sometimes seem necessary
to be a London cab driver.

It would seem sensible to involve those who best understand
the role when setting up competences, but this may not always
happen, and it is only quite recently that British teachers have
begun to be consulted about defining their own professional competence. Previously, competence statements were largely imposed
from above, to the disgust of writers like Thompson (1992), who
gave her article on the new secondary teacher competences (DfE
1992) the subtitle 'Why chickens should decide the sauce in which
they are to be served'. In such circumstances it was clear that
part of the real function of competences was one of 'top-down'
social control, and in this respect, the competence movement
itself provides a neat illustration of the importance of the wider
social context in which teachers work.

Developing societies have needed to set up schools as separate, formal places of learning with their own distinct sets of rules
and roles, while the functions that schools are expected to perform both reflect and shape the values of the wider culture in
which they operate (Bruner 1996). Cognitive psychologists are
therefore shifting from a view of learning that sees the child as

an isolated explorer, to one that sees learning as mediated through social encounters, and we will consider the social contexts of successful learning and teaching in more depth in Chapter 5.

Moving on

This first chapter has introduced some of the main themes of the book and has tried to show how successful learning and teaching cannot be discussed purely in terms of competent behaviour, but also need to take into account cognitive processes, attitudes and social contexts. The next chapter will begin to look at the cognitive processes involved in teaching and learning.

2

Teaching, learning and Napoleon's socks: cognition and success

Cameo 1

Mrs S. is talking to her Year 5 class and is sure that Janet is daydreaming as usual, not listening to a word. To capture her attention Mrs S. suddenly asks, 'Janet, what did I just say?' Much to her annoyance, Janet calmly repeats the last few words said, then returns to her daydream!

Cameo 2

Jason, a Year 3 boy, is reading aloud to Ms K. He gets to a sentence which introduces a new character called Silas, and the last word in the sentence is this new name. He is completely stuck and, after offering a bit of help, Ms K. eventually tells him what it says. He repeats it correctly. The very first word in the next sentence is 'Silas'. Jason is completely stuck again.

Cameo 3

When our first son was three years old and was having one of the temper tantrums so embarrassingly familiar to the parents of toddlers, he would often shout the word 'chance' to vent his frustration at the unfairness of life. Though we were not particularly worried about this (he could after all have shouted much worse things), we were rather puzzled until we realized why he did it.

(The explanation to Cameo 3 will be revealed later on in the chapter.)

Cognition and the teacher

Teachers as experts

Modesty aside, teachers *are* experts. Many primary teachers feel slightly uncomfortable with such a label, especially given the barrage of criticism they seem to get from all sides. But teachers are experts, at least in comparison with their pupils and the public at large, as authorities on a wide range of topics from the water cycle to rotational symmetry and from electrical circuits to the Anglo-Saxons. Teachers are also experts in understanding and managing children, and these two sorts of expertise represent both the content and processes of learning.

Although this chapter will focus on cognitive processes, we must not emphasize these at the expense of content and knowledge because both are obviously vital, and we must acknowledge that the teacher is not just a facilitator of children's learning but is also an expert with valuable information and skills to pass on. In fact, psychologists have studied highly skilled performance in various domains ranging from chess to Morse code, and their research is relevant to the role of the teacher as expert.

One finding is that most experts tend to have expertise only in their own particular area or domain – they do not necessarily need a high level of 'general intelligence', particularly since such a concept is problematic anyway, as we shall see later in the chapter. For instance, an expert chess player seems to require an almost superhuman memory capacity to remember and predict thousands of possible moves, yet will have only an average memory for other sorts of information. The explanation again highlights the interplay between knowledge and processes: experts typically use their detailed knowledge to think in large 'chunks' rather than in small, discrete bits of information (Hatano 1994). As a demonstration, even an expert reader would find the following series of letters laborious to copy down and difficult to remember:

Nwplr aao ydrkc eaeo oeo wlnsns

The ability to read fluently is of little help here, but if the same letters were arranged into 'nonsense words', they would be easier to copy and could be remembered fairly accurately (if someone really wanted to!):

Nena slare lars pow woyd seck

The second example is easier because the letters are in larger units which can be pronounced – a reader can look quickly at 'slare' for instance, pronounce the sound as a single 'nonsense word' in their head and reconstruct the sequence of letters from that. But if the same letters were rearranged again into a meaningful sentence, even one which nobody had never seen before, the whole sequence could be recalled after a single glance:

Napoleon always wore one red sock

In the final example, we are able to use our expert knowledge, not of the Napoleonic dress code, but simply of words and meanings, to form one large meaningful 'chunk', and if we had to recall the letters, we would *re-create* them from this large chunk. In a way, we wouldn't *remember* that third letter was 'p', we would *deduce* that it was.

This notion of expertise does present a problem if we apply it to teaching, however. For example, it is true that children can learn something about the value of reading simply by noticing that their teacher reads sometimes, and techniques like ERIC (Everyone Reads In Class) and USSR (Uninterrupted Sustained Silent Reading) are based on this idea. But if experts actually think and perform differently from novices, then for many activities it may not be enough for the teacher to be an expert or model and for the children to observe and then try to copy them – the classic 'sitting with Nellie'. This is particularly apparent when the observable part of the expert performance is the result of a lot of thinking. A novice could not learn to play chess simply by watching an expert move the pieces, although their observable behaviour would be the same (at least to a non chess player). Even a child could soon learn to put on an intense expression, then move a piece with flair, start the timer and sit back looking smug, but they wouldn't understand the thinking behind the moves. In order to teach someone else, the expert must also be able to make their expertise explicit so that it is available to learners.

One way to do this is for the teacher to talk through what they are doing, and 'expert protocols' seem to be helpful to learners (e.g. David and Palincsar 1994). For instance, a teacher might not simply model for a child how to look up a word in the dictionary by letting the child see them do it, but could also talk through what they are doing, asking themselves questions, exaggerating important parts of the activity that might not be noticed and generally *not* behaving like an expert whose performance is highly fluent and automatic:

> OK, I want to find what 'catastrophe' means. What's the first letter? Oh yes, 'c'. [points to it] Let's think of the alphabet: a, b, c. C is near the beginning of the alphabet, so I'll open the dictionary near the beginning. [Runs finger over pages and opens dictionary slowly] What word is at the top of this page? [Pointing] 'basil'. That begins with 'b'. [points to it]. A, **b**, c. I want 'c' for 'catastrophe', so I need to look further on . . . [etc.]

Interestingly, some experts may find it quite difficult to do this. They may be so immersed in their subject or perform so automatically that such a rigmarole may seem tedious and even alien to them. Perhaps they genuinely cannot see what the learner's problem might be, or may not be able to slow down and explain exactly what they are doing at each stage without their own performance deteriorating, or at least changing, causing frustrating problems for both teacher and learner. Anyone who has had golf lessons or has tried to teach someone else to drive will know this feeling! Because of such problems, it could even be argued that a high level of subject knowledge, usually seen as the first priority in lists of teacher competencies, is *not* always helpful in teaching unless the expert is also able to 'step outside' their own fluent performance and make it available to the novice.

Teachers and psychology

The first chapter emphasized the active nature of children's learning, in contrast to the classic 'empty vessels' view in which children's minds are seen as mere containers passively waiting to be filled with knowledge. Similarly, the first section of this chapter has proposed a view of teacher expertise as depending on the active, fluent processing of information which needs to be made explicitly available if learners are to benefit from it. The notions of the active learner and the reflective practitioner are not merely ones which most psychologists would agree with, but are also views which most British teachers would now accept, or at least recognize.

However, these views make far more complex demands on the teacher than the traditional 'transmission' model ever did. Reflective practitioners cannot simply deliver pearls of wisdom to a grateful and passive audience, and the implications for teachers of such an active and child-centred view of learning can be quite disturbing. One response is to give up trying to teach at all. After years of classroom experience, Holt (1991) concluded that learning is not the product of teaching because when he started teaching less, the children started learning more! He thus proposed that teachers should just be available to offer 'slight assistance' – and then only when children ask for it.

While this may seem an attractive proposition to overworked teachers, it is unrealistic in the face of increased accountability, Ofsted inspections and the demands of the National Curriculum. More generally, it is true that children do need to construct knowledge for themselves in order to understand properly, but they do not do so in a vacuum. As we shall see in Chapter 5, psychologists are increasingly recognizing that almost all knowledge is socially constructed and transmitted, and most of the things children learn are things that adults already know (Light *et al.* 1991). Ideally, of course, we would like children to discover spontaneously for themselves the very things that we just happen to have planned for them to learn on that particular occasion, but this is not an argument for simply sitting around in the hope that they will do so.

The alternative may appear challenging, however. If we recognize the importance of each child's construction of understanding, how can a teacher possibly take into consideration the vast array of abilities, prior knowledge, skills, interests, personalities, attitudes and motivations that confront them in a typical class of children? It is tempting to fall back on more 'traditional' transmission methods of teaching, especially since such approaches seem more in line with the requirement to deliver a fixed, subject-based and overcrowded National Curriculum, and a return to more class teaching has certainly been advocated by some. If a teacher is required to teach 30 children about river erosion in the next half hour, stopping for too long to consider their individual understandings may seem a unaffordable luxury, for all she or he may approve of it in theory. Of course it would be better for each of them to find out for themselves, but the teacher might worry that some would never manage it, some might already understand it, and others would take all week, by which time he or she has to have 'delivered' the circulation of the blood, basic probability theory and a brief history of the Benin.

The rest of this chapter will therefore look at some of the things psychologists have discovered about children's learning, and will try to consider realistically what the implications might be, not for further research in the psychology laboratory, but for harassed teachers in the classroom.

Cognition and the child

The child as learner: a cognitive view

Cameo 3 at the beginning of this chapter described how our young son used to shout 'chance' when feeling particularly frustrated. This was because our response to his more outrageous demands had sometimes been the rather harsh phrase 'no chance', so that when he shouted 'chance' he was putting his point of view in what was a perfectly reasonable and logical way. He had recognized a grammatical rule about negatives and had spontaneously applied it in a way that he could not possibly just have copied from us or anybody else. In doing so, his behaviour neatly illustrated a view of children's learning which has been promoted by cognitive psychologists for several decades. This view portrays successful learning as a set of overlapping processes, where learners actively seek out new information, select from it, transform it, impose meaning on it and evaluate it in the light of what they already know. Such cognitive activity is crucial because we are very limited in the amount of information we can attend to, perceive or hold in our memories at any one time. For instance, most psychologists would now agree that:

- We can really only attend to one thing at a time in any depth, though we do process other things that are going on very lightly, so that we can switch our attention if something more important crops up.
- We can attend to the same thing for only a short time before our attention wanders – our attention span even as adults is limited. However, even though children's attention spans are generally shorter, they can sometimes attend to something with great intensity and for a considerable length of time.

Even though children's attention span is generally shorter, they can sometimes attend to something with great intensity and for a considerable length of time

- When we look at something, we don't actually take in the whole thing at a glance. Our eyes move rapidly over it, taking lots of tiny 'snapshots' of details every second, and we rely on our past experience, knowledge and expectations to make up for the fragmentary information we receive.
- We can remember only a very small amount of information for a very short time in our short-term memory before it fades away, unless we deliberately make an effort to remember it. Otherwise, the amount we can hold is limited to a few discrete items for a few seconds.
- Information thus has to pass through a series of bottlenecks in order to be stored in long-term memory more or less permanently, and it might seem almost impossible for us to learn anything given such limitations!

Figure 2.1 One teacher drew this on the spine of her lesson plan file. Can you tell what it is?

For instance, if you look at Figure 2.1 you may well not recognize immediately what it is. In fact, it is the word 'file' written vertically in white on a black background. Even from this very simple example, we can learn a lot:

- Why do some people not recognize it immediately? The answer is that our past experience of pictures tells us that if something black is surrounded by white space, the picture is of the black thing and the white is the background. In this case, however, past experience misleads us. Children too may sometimes fail to understand something because they apply their past experience inappropriately, or because they make assumptions based on misconceptions.
- When we do recognize it, we do so very suddenly, in a flash of insight, rather than deciding to try out a different approach and slowly coming to realize what it is. And once we have recognized it, it becomes almost impossible *not* to see it, even after a considerable time. The same thing can happen with children's learning. Most teachers treasure the moment when a child suddenly says, 'Oh yes, I get it now!' as one of the

most rewarding experiences in teaching, and if the child really has gained a sudden insight into something, they are very unlikely to forget it.

- The illustration also reveals some important points about the nature of memory itself. Imagine two people, one of whom has recognized the picture and one who has not, both being asked to reproduce it from memory. For the one who does not know what it is, the task is virtually impossible because trying to reproduce all the complicated black shapes completely overloads their capacity for processing information. (They would also probably feel negative about the task and prefer not to do it because it would be a waste of time to try.)

- In contrast, someone who has recognized it would feel quite confident about their ability to reproduce it, but they would not actually draw it from memory at all! Instead, they would consider the mental model they have, and recreate the picture from that, perhaps saying something like, 'It was the word 'FILE' in white, on a black background, *so it must have looked like this*'. For instance, when people do try to reproduce the picture, they often shade in a strip of black at the top and bottom, or forget to include the serifs on the letters because their mental model was not totally accurate. This is very much how memory works, and children often show that they too have imperfect mental models. For example, if a child thinks of the letter 'b' as 'a ball and a stick', but also thinks of the letter 'd' in the same way, they will confuse the two because their mental models are not distinctive.

The first cameo, about Janet's ability to repeat what the teacher had just said in spite of her apparent inattention, also tells us something about the nature of memory and attention. Here, although she had been mainly concentrating on her daydream, she was still just about aware of other things going on; calling her name grabbed her attention and allowed her to switch to the fleeting memory of what she had just heard. If asked what the teacher had said 20 seconds earlier, she would have no idea because it would have faded from her short-term memory without her having thought about it enough to recall the gist of what the teacher had said.

This 'cognitive' view of learning implies that what we can take in from the outside world is both restricted and fragmentary, and if we consider that the limitations faced by children may be even more severe, it seems such a ridiculously gloomy view – after all, our pupils do manage to learn things occasionally! However, adults have developed strategies to overcome these limitations so effectively that they are not normally aware of them, and a major role for teachers will therefore be to help children to do the same in order to become successful learners.

In fact, to become independent as learners, children need to develop not only cognitive strategies, but also the ability to select and apply them appropriately and to monitor their success. In turn, such higher-level skills require an awareness of our own cognitive processes which is one of the hallmarks of successful mature thinking – an awareness which psychologists call 'meta-cognition', mentioned in the first chapter.

Having very briefly outlined the general view of learning accepted by most psychologists, we can now look in a little more detail at three aspects which are of particular importance to teachers:

- accessing children's prior knowledge;
- making children's learning more explicit;
- being aware of individual differences.

Accessing children's prior knowledge

If prior knowledge plays such an important part in children's learning, then before embarking on a new topic, it will be vital to find out what they already know. This sounds obvious, but it is easy to assume that what a teacher thinks the children have been taught in the past is identical to what the children actually know now! This first step should also include activating any relevant knowledge they may have without recognizing it, and getting rid of any misconceptions. 'Knowledge' is also being used very broadly here, to include not only factual information but also the children's attitudes and feelings, which we will discuss more in Chapter 4.

One way to do this is by some sort of 'baseline' test, and this is what happens on many behavioural programmes which use a fixed sequence for children to work through. However, there is a danger in assuming that learning develops in a smooth, sequential way with each child going through the same steps, and in any case, finding what the children already know need not necessarily take the form of a test. Informal questioning is a common way of beginning a topic, but an alternative is for the children to be encouraged to ask the teacher questions for a change! This is quite an unusual social activity, and both teachers and children may find it difficult at first. It is not productive for children to regard question-asking as something only done by teachers, nor is it necessary for teachers to feel threatened by 'awkward' questions, since children can learn a lot from seeing how an adult copes with not knowing something. They may also feel more involved in the topic if they have generated questions for themselves.

Another approach is for the children to talk in groups and share their knowledge, then present their ideas to the rest of the class. It might involve writing, but 'mind maps' (see below and Buzan 1995) offer an alternative, with or without some initial structure from the teacher. It is important to recognize that such opening activities are not valuable time wasted instead of teaching! The more the teacher understands about what the children already know, the more effective his or her own input will be, and the more the children have thought about something first, the more motivated they are likely to be. If the teacher can highlight some misconceptions, she or he will be paving the way for what many psychologists see as 'real' learning (e.g. Sotto 1994).

Making children's learning more explicit

The idea of getting children to record what they already know can be extended to writing about what they think they have actually learned, using a 'learning journal' or 'learning log' (Dougill and Knott 1988), and such writing can serve several purposes:

- By making the children's perceptions explicit, it can reveal to the teacher any gaps or misconceptions.
- Many teachers agree that we really understand something only when we have to teach it and thus to make it explicit to somebody else. Similarly, having to make something explicit in writing can in itself sometimes help learners to understand better.
- Equally, writing something down can act as a very helpful review, and most psychologists agree that the process of reviewing what we have learned means that we are more likely to remember it in the long term.

- It also helps children to take responsibility for their own learning and can raise self-esteem by showing progress (Fisher 1995).

Swan and White (1994) present an example of such an approach which they called 'the Thinking Books'. Here, 8-year-olds wrote down at the end of each day something they had learned, along with any questions. The teacher wrote a brief response, often in the form of another question, setting up a dialogue in writing. It soon became apparent that the children often latched on to 'surface features' such as vivid examples, without necessarily understanding, and that there were misconceptions which would hinder learning but which might not have otherwise been picked up. (One child for example confused Captain Cook with Captain Hook!) The children found it difficult at first, and wrote about what they had done rather than what they had learned, but eventually they began to think about their learning and to take more control over it. One child even developed his own headings:

- What I learned.
- What use it may be.
- When I have used it before.
- What I already knew about it.
- My questions.

Significantly, there were still effects being reported five years later, by teachers who found that these children asked more questions than others and were more able to see links between different things they had learned.

The format need not be conventional writing, of course. Another way of collecting and organizing thoughts is the 'mind map', also known as the 'topic web' or the 'spider chart' or by various other names. Here, ideas or information are organized graphically rather than in conventional written form. Though the result may seem messy and idiosyncratic, it may actually represent the way our minds work more accurately than normal writing. Primary teachers often use this format for planning projects but may not have thought of introducing the method to children, even though those who think in more spatial and visual ways might find it particularly helpful (see below). Mind maps could be a good way for individual children or groups to collect together what they already know about a topic, to share with the teacher or with other children, and they could then be added to as work on the project progressed, alongside or even sometimes replacing more conventional forms of writing. Fisher (1995) presents an interesting discussion of these techniques and their use in the classroom.

Being aware of individual differences

The idea that people prefer different ways of thinking is not a new one, though cognitive psychologists have in the past tended to concentrate less on individual differences than on trying to discover general 'laws' about thinking. Some people think best through visual images, others through the auditory system and still others kinaesthetically or through movement, and a lively if controversial approach, neuro-linguistic programming, proposes that such preferences can be directly observed in people's eye movements (O'Connor and Seymour 1993).

The two hemispheres of the brain tend to work in different ways, though many activities involve both halves and the distinction between the two is not as simple as was first thought. Even so, some individuals do seem to think in rather more in 'right-brain' ways and others in 'left-brain' ways (e.g. Smith 1996). Some of the main distinctions are outlined in Table 2.1.

In many ways, left-brain thinking would therefore seem to be more valued in the core subjects of the National Curriculum, and some of the ideas mentioned in this chapter (such as presenting advance organizers or using mind maps) could be particularly helpful for children who prefer right-brain styles of thinking.

Other psychologists have proposed even more complex individual differences in thinking preferences. One of the best-known accounts of such individual differences which has recently become popular again is Gardner's (1983) notion of 'multiple

Table 2.1 Differences between the two sides of the brain

Left brain	Right brain
Items in sequences	Spatial arrangements
Language	Images
Number	Music
Building up part to a whole	Breaking whole down into parts

intelligences'. Briefly, Gardner proposed seven distinct forms of intelligence:

- Linguistic.
- Mathematical.
- Visual/spatial.
- Musical.
- Interpersonal (relating to others).
- Intrapersonal (self-understanding).
- Kinaesthetic.

It clearly is not usual for a child to have, say, high musical intelligence and nothing else. Each person can be seen as having a different profile, with strengths and weaknesses across the whole range, so that individual differences become very complicated.

The final part of this chapter will look more closely at the contexts in which school teaching and learning take place together, and will suggest some more ways of putting into practice the ideas already discussed.

Cognition in context

Learning processes and learning products

At the heart of the dilemma facing teachers is a conflict between the content-based requirements of what teachers have to *teach* and the process-based understanding of how children *learn*. The greatest challenge in trying to understand, assess or improve cognitive processes is obviously that they are hidden and can only be inferred from what people say or do. This is partly why they tend to be ignored in favour of the behaviour of the children or the content of the curriculum, especially if aspects of behaviour or content can be expressed as competences and assessed.

However, care is needed here. Historically, education is full of dichotomies such as 'progressive versus traditional' or 'phonics versus word recognition' that are ultimately unhelpful because they simplify the complex realities of learning for the sake of a nice clear-cut argument in which everybody can join. The previous chapter thus suggested that it was unproductive to set up a dichotomy between 'good' teachers as warm but eccentric and 'bad' teachers as cold but competent, and it would be equally unhelpful here to set up a dichotomy between a 'good' emphasis on learning processes and a 'bad' one on learning products or content. (For a detailed analysis of the relationship between knowledge and cognitive processes, see Meadows (1993) or Howe (1991)).

Advance organizers

One very general strategy that teachers can try is to make these hidden processes more explicit, and some ways of doing this have already been discussed with regard to children's thinking (such as learning logs or mind maps) and teachers' own expertise (such as protocols, as in the example of looking up a word in a dictionary, discussed earlier in this chapter). Extending this idea a little, just as it is vital to know about children's prior knowledge before trying to teach them something new, it can be very helpful for children to be aware of the sorts of prior knowledge which their teacher thinks they will need. One obvious idea is first to present 'the big picture' or an 'advance organizer' – a preliminary outline of what the whole session or topic will be about. This will be particularly helpful to children who find it easier to think in terms of 'wholes' rather than serially (Smith 1996), though it will help all of them to see the purpose of the activity and to relate it to their existing knowledge, both of which are vital for successful learning.

Teaching children strategies

Making children's prior knowledge and learning more open to the teacher is very useful, but it is also important to consider *how* children may go about learning. One approach which has met with some success has simply been to try to teach children to use learning strategies which they would not have used spontaneously. This can be particularly effective for children with learning difficulties who appear to have very few strategies of their own, and who simply don't know what to do when presented with a list of items to learn. For instance, given the weekly list of spellings, they may just look vaguely at the words in the hope that they will somehow float off the page into the brain. A strategy such as 'look/cover/write/check' can therefore be very helpful, particularly if they are given more guidance about the first step and shown various ways to 'internalize' the correct spelling before testing themselves (Merry 1992).

The general picture which emerges from research into teaching children to use strategies is that they can be taught to use specific techniques such as mnemonics, using particular materials under particular circumstances, with considerable success. However, they may well not spontaneously transfer these skills to new situations or content (Levin 1993). It seems that knowing about the strategies is not enough: children also need to learn how to choose strategies and monitor their use, so that feedback about their success is more likely to result in the strategy being applied again (McShane 1991).

Improving general thinking skills

There have also been some attempts to design programmes which emphasize 'pure' processes and whose content is deliberately not related specifically to the curriculum. De Bono, for instance, has produced a series of lively ideas to promote creative or lateral thinking (for a review, see Hunter-Grundin 1985). Similarly, Feuerstein's Instrumental Enrichment programme claims to be 'content-free' and to improve general cognitive functioning, particularly in children with learning difficulties. Perhaps surprisingly, Feuerstein's own books tend to be rather difficult to read, but a good summary is provided by Sharron and Coulter (1994). The programme has met with some success (see Burden and Florek 1990) and supporters say that the lack of similarity to curriculum materials not only motivates children who associate traditional materials with failure, but also encourages more general thinking skills. Other programmes include The Primary Thinking Skills Project and The Top Ten Thinking Tactics (see Foster 1994a and 1994b, and Hawkins 1995 for discussions and reviews).

However, some writers have claimed that such general or 'content-free' materials are ineffective. Thus the authors of the *Somerset Thinking Skills Course Handbook*, while recognizing their debt to the ideas of Feuerstein, describe his materials as:

a series of novel, abstract activities in a contextually bare medium freed from traditional subject constraints, which offers the potential for maximum generalisation . . . However, in many instances both pupils and teachers found it difficult to generalise from abstract contexts to real life.

(Blagg *et al.* 1988: 30)

Similarly, Bransford *et al.* (1989) criticized programmes aimed at developing general thinking skills because they cannot take into account the different thinking and learning strategies required by different 'domains' or subjects. Gardner *et al.* (1994) studied the development of 'practical intelligence for school' (PIFS) and concluded that better results were achieved by the use of 'infused' courses closely linked to the school curriculum, rather than 'stand alone' courses designed to develop general skills such as self-management.

Cognitive processes and planning activities

So how is it possible to recognize cognitive processes a little more in actual teaching? One idea which is in keeping with the current theme of making these processes explicit is to use a simple way of recording not only the content of what is given to the children, but also the processes which may be involved. To get the most from this, it will help to take a sheet of paper and draw three columns.

- To begin with, consider the sorts of things which could be presented to children, without being too specific, and write down as many as possible in the first (left-hand) column. Examples would be pictures or tape recordings.
- Next think about the range of general activities which children could be asked to carry out in response to whatever they have been given. Again, don't try to be too specific – suggestions might be drawing a diagram or cutting something out. Make up a list in the third (right-hand) column.
- Finally, the hard bit! Look at the two lists and think what processes might be going on in the child's head, between the inputs in the first column and the actions in the third one, and note them down in the second (middle) column. Examples might be comparing or sequencing. This is much harder, for the reasons mentioned earlier.

Now have a look at Table 2.2 at the end of this chapter. The lists it shows may be very different from those you produced, but such differences in content are less important than the process of drawing up the lists, and they in any case represent individual differences in how people think.

So how can the three lists be used? There are two basic ways. The first is for teachers to compare the lists in Table 2.2 with their own ideas and to think about any differences, then to analyze some of the activities they like to use most often, trying to see how these ideas fit the columns. Most people tend to rely on the same few ideas, and their choices usually represent their own favourite ways of thinking and learning, though these may of course not be the best ones for all children.

Second, the columns can help teachers to devise different sorts of activities that they probably would normally not have thought of. An unusual route through the three columns can be deliberately chosen, even by sticking a pin in each column in turn to see if it produces an idea using that particular pathway for some work actually being planned. Alternatively, colleagues, family or friends may take a sadistic delight in trying to think up tricky combinations! Of course, some combinations may be downright impossible or simply too bizarre to use, but a little practice and imagination should produce some lively activities which may well appeal to children who might have found more conventional methods less easy or interesting. Similarly, changing just one column (usually the first or the third) gives ideas for differentiation. For a detailed example using the theme of a robbery, see Kitson and Merry (1992).

The three columns (input/processing/output) are compatible with the general approach of cognitive psychology outlined in this chapter and with the particular ideas of psychologists like Feuerstein (see Sharron and Coulter 1994). They should encourage more emphasis on processes as well as products and create a wider range of activities than might otherwise have been considered, not through special artificial materials, but within the content of the actual curriculum.

Moving on

This chapter has outlined some major ideas derived from cognitive psychology, and considered how they might be applied to teaching. In particular, it has tried to show how limited the processes of attention, perception and remembering really are, and how as adults we have learned to overcome these limitations. We normally take these processes for granted, yet as teachers, it is not only helpful for us to be aware of them in our own thinking and teaching, but also to recognize how they affect children's learning. However, children are clearly not born with all these cognitive processing skills in place, and the next chapter will look at how they develop.

Table 2.2   Examples of different inputs, processes and outputs

Inputs or stimuli	Processes (invisible)	Outputs or products (observable)
First-hand experiences	Recognizing	Moving/arranging
Real objects	Remembering	Completing
Models	Matching	Highlighting
Video/audio tape	Comparing	Connecting
Pictures	Finding/selecting	Drawing
Other people	Sequencing	Constructing
Maps/diagrams	Categorizing	Identifying
Words/text	Analyzing	Answering/asking
Tables	Synthesizing	questions
Speech	Transforming (e.g. words into images or vice versa)	Telling Acting Writing
	Predicting	
	Applying	
	Inferencing	
	Imagining	
	Hypothesizing	
	Evaluating	

Source: Kitson and Merry (1992).

3

Cognitive development: teaching and the 'P' word

Cameo 1

Mr N. is learning how to type. At first, he finds it very hard to remember where each letter is, and has to scan the entire keyboard to find it. After a while, however, he begins to remember roughly where some of the letters are. Moreover, he finds that his fingers begin to move more automatically through the letter sequences of some very common words like 'the' or 'that', or common sequences like 'ion', treating them more like one larger 'chunk' rather than separate letters.

Cameo 2

Aliya is investigating objects that float and sink, and has chosen a range of materials including a nail, a key, a magnet, some balsa wood, some polystyrene and a bit of paper. Discussing her findings with her teacher Mrs Y., she concludes that metal things don't float. Mrs Y. knows that Aliya has recently been to France on the ferry, and, after talking about that, she innocently asks Aliya what the ship was made of. With a little prompting, she answers 'iron', but doesn't make any connection with her experiment. Mrs Y. points out the discrepancy and, after a moment's thought, Aliya replies that there was a lot of wood and plastic on the ferry too. Mrs Y. then produces her trump card – an aluminium foil carton, which Aliya already knows is made of metal. When asked, she predicts that it will not float, and seems surprised when it does. However, she then thinks for a moment, and says triumphantly, 'Ah yes,

but that's not *proper* metal!' Mrs Y. suggests that she
continues experimenting, and moves on, defeated,
to the next table.

Introduction

Chapter 2 began with a section on the teacher, encouraging
readers to reflect on their own thinking before considering how
children learn, and in most of the other chapters there is a section
with a focus on the teacher which invites readers to think about
how the topic of the chapter relates to them as an adult and a
teacher as well as to children and their learning. As this chapter
is about child development, most of the chapter is about
children, and the next section focusing on the teacher is rather
shorter than in the other chapters.

The teacher

Teaching an old dog new tricks?

It is useful to reflect first on how even adult thinking sometimes
can develop, especially if it is accepted that learning is life-long –
most teachers would agree that the day they think they can stop
learning is the day they might as well give up completely! For
instance, readers could reflect on a new skill they have learned
as an adult. It could be something learned some time ago, though
it might be more vivid if it was more recent. Whatever is chosen,
it will probably involve both observable actions and mental processes, though the apparent importance of the two may vary. It
could be a very physical skill like a new sport or playing a musical
instrument, though these obviously also require some sort of
thinking too. Conversely, it could be something requiring mainly
mental effort such as learning a new language, though even here
there may be a physical component such as shaping one's mouth
to produce the correct pronunciation. Ideally, it should also be
something where the reader feels that he or she has moved beyond the stage of being a total beginner. Comparing first attempts
with current performance raises questions such as:

- How would an observer know that the performance is quite proficient?
- Is there anything that beginners do which experts don't?
- Is there anything experts do which beginners don't?
- How does the speed of someone's performance increase?

It may be difficult to say, though there is one interesting technique to try if the chosen activity involves obvious motor skills. If it is possible, try performing the task left-handed (left-handed readers should try doing it right-handed of course). This works particularly well with something like playing the guitar, and learners who are getting discouraged can be reminded that they really have progressed.

Another aspect of how adult thinking develops is shown in Cameo 1, which illustrates the development of larger 'chunks' of information and skills discussed in the previous chapter, when it was shown that real words are much easier to deal with than strings of random letters. As with reading, such chunks enable performance to become much more automatic and fluent.

Thinking in different ways

Apart from using 'chunking', learners may also sometimes actually change the whole way they think about something, even as adults. Here is an example. Try to picture in your mind's eye a huge piece of thin tissue paper, entirely covering a whole football pitch. Now imagine folding it in half and slitting along the fold to make it lie flat. Really try to imagine doing this, then repeating it 50 times, folding the paper in half and slitting the fold each time. Very roughly, how thick would the resulting pile of sheets be? Really try to imagine doing it, to get an idea of the answer.

Now try a different approach to the same problem. Folding the sheet once produces two thicknesses. Folding again makes four thicknesses, and eight the next time. The number of thicknesses doubles each time, or to put it another way, the number of thicknesses increases from 1 to 2, to 2^2 then 2^3 then 2^4 etc., so after 50 folds there would be 2^{50} thicknesses – a colossal number. Even if it takes a hundred sheets of the paper to make a centimetre, the number of thicknesses is so huge that the pile would be millions of kilometres thick!

So what happened here, and what does it show? Picturing the situation in the mind's eye and imagining how thick the pile would be restricts thinking to a more primitive form involving only visual information and past experience. These are totally inadequate for the problem, and most people underestimate the answer considerably because they simply cannot imagine such a huge figure. However, when the problem is put in a different way, people are no longer restricted to visual images and are able to use their understanding of mathematics and to use symbols like 2^3 to calculate the answer, or at least to appreciate that it would be enormous. In a way, symbols thus allow more sophisticated learners to escape from the limitations of what they could imagine visually, and the ability to change to thinking in this way is crucial in normal child development.

Cameo 1 is about learning a new skill such as typing, and showed one way in which adult performance can develop fluency through the use of larger 'chunks' of behaviour or thought. The example of folding the paper illustrated a major change in children's thinking which can also sometimes be seen in adults. Bearing these in mind, this chapter now turns to look at some influential ideas about how children's thinking develops.

The child

'Big theories' of child development

Before proceeding any further, let's get something important out of the way: Piaget. There, I've said it: the 'P' word! For many years, developmental psychology was dominated by the work of one man – Jean Piaget, and the very mention of his name is still enough to strike terror into the hearts of some who trained to teach some time ago! However, particularly since his death, there has been an increased recognition of some of the limitations and problems with his theories, and the ideas of other psychologists such as Bruner and Vygotsky have gained more attention. It may come as a relief to hear that it is not the intention of this chapter to describe and compare these theorists, as summaries and discussions of their work are readily available elsewhere (e.g. Butterworth and Harris 1994; Das Gupta and Richardson 1995).

The most detailed discussion and comparison of all three major theories is still that by Wood (1988).

In the last few years, there have been no major general developmental theories, with the exception of Donaldson (1992). Psychologists have concentrated more on particular areas such as the development of writing or drawing, or even on specific tasks within those domains (see Chapter 2). McShane (1991) therefore distinguishes between 'bottom-up' approaches which focus on such specifics, and 'top-down' theories which try to find general laws for all human development, concerning what he calls the whole 'cognitive architecture'. Rather than providing another summary of these 'big theories', this chapter will indicate some common trends in psychologists' understanding of cognitive development, and their implications for teachers.

A general shift in thinking

Although the big top-down theories differ from each other in important ways, they do have some things in common, including the notion of a general shift in children's conceptualizing. Described and explained in different ways, this general shift can be seen as a development away from having to rely on external concrete experience to an ability to deal in more abstract ideas. This trend can be very briefly summarized as it appears in four of the most influential theories:

Piaget certainly saw a major development from 'concrete operations' to 'formal operations'. Early thinking is dominated by sensory information, and the capacity for abstract thought only emerges later. Thus, in probably his most famous set of demonstrations, Piaget maintained that young children think that the volume of liquid in a jar does actually change if it is poured into another jar where it *looks* different.

Bruner (1973) described three ways of representing the world, though he did not see them as replacing each other as we develop, and noted that as adults we may revert to more primitive forms of thinking if confronted by a novel problem. The stages are:

- *Enactive representation* where young children learn best if they have actual objects to manipulate.

Young children learn best if they have actual objects to manipulate

- *Iconic representation* which involves the use of pictures and mental images to replace the real objects.
- *Symbolic representation* where the learner can think in symbols which bear no relation to real objects or situations.

The illustration about folding the tissue paper illustrates these three levels of representation. Clearly, anyone who could only solve the problem by acting it out would be doomed to fail, and the solution is almost as impossible to estimate through the use of visual imagery. But someone who understands the mathematics behind the problem can use symbols to escape from the limitations of action or sensory experience.

Vygotsky also saw an important shift from a reliance on actions performed in the outside world, particularly with the support of more mature learners and their language, to an ability to internalize actions and language as thoughts. Although it is expressed rather differently, this development from action to thought can be seen in parallel to the ideas of Piaget and Bruner.

Donaldson (1992) has more recently outlined a general shift through four modes, with thinking moving away from being embedded in particular contexts. Because the ideas may appear rather complex, and because the theory is perhaps not yet as well-known as the others, a brief example of each is given below:

- *Point mode* where thinking can only take place in the here and now (e.g. 'My Dad's got more chips than I have').
- *Line mode* where the child still thinks in specific terms, but can consider different times and places (e.g. 'He got more chips than I did last week as well').
- *Construct mode* which no longer needs to refer to any particular place or time (e.g. 'He *always* gets more chips than I do').
- *Transcendent mode* which is completely free of space and time (e.g. 'Big people have a better life than little people!').

The fact that the concrete examples of Donaldson's modes make them easier to understand suggests that the general shift is, as Bruner proposed, an important one which still has validity for adults. In order to explore this shift and other aspects of cognitive development, the next part of this chapter will consider two important factors – *what* actually develops, and *how* changes occur.

What develops

There seem to be four main candidates:

- Capacity
- Knowledge
- Available strategies
- Strategy control.

Capacity

Smith (1996) presents an interesting discussion of how the development of the brain can be related to classroom learning, and in one sense, capacity could be seen as increasing as more pathways are formed between neurons. The physical development of the brain is very significant in young children's learning, but most psychologists would agree that cognitive development in the school years does not occur simply because the actual capacity of the brain increases.

In a very influential and entertaining paper written many years ago, Miller (1956) proposed a 'central limitation' on our ability to process information, so that if we have to deal with more than about seven (plus or minus two) discrete pieces of information at once, we cannot cope. As an illustration, think back to the sentence about Napoleon in the previous chapter (see page 29). Which of these words appeared in it?

sack sock soak sick suck

Now consider the sequence where the same 28 letters were arranged in pronounceable 'nonsense' words, and try to say which of these appeared in that sequence:

slars slar lers sler lars

This is much harder, and it is probably impossible to say which one of these appeared when the letters were rearranged randomly:

eaeo oeao eoao oaea aoea

(Anyone who can do this would be well advised to get out of education immediately and go on the stage!)

The explanation for the different performances does therefore not lie in pure capacity, since all three sequences had the same number of letters, but in the way that capacity was *used*. If the letters are arranged in a way that means something to the reader, there is no need to try to remember them as 28 individual items, which is far beyond memory capacity. Instead, they can be recalled as half a dozen separate words. Thus, if the reader can recall just the first word, they can *deduce* that the third letter was 'p'. Interestingly, of course, to a beginner reader who could recognize individual letters but not words, all three sentences would be equally difficult, just as it would make no difference to a Westerner if some Chinese symbols they were trying to recall were arranged in a meaningful or a random order.

Knowledge

As was shown in the earlier discussion of expertise, prior knowledge is crucial because it enables information to be organized
and made meaningful so that learners can get round the problems posed by limited processing capacity. Yet, perhaps because
they tend to be more interested in processes than in content,
some cognitive psychologists have in the past tended to play
down the relative importance of knowledge:

> A few years ago, psychologists like myself who favoured a
> broadly cognitive approach to education thought we knew
> what had to be done to help children and adults to be better
> learners. Essentially, our advice to teachers was to stop cram-
> ming the children's heads with factual information and con-
> centrate on helping them learn how to learn. So we argued
> that instead of attaching importance to mere knowledge, the
> emphasis should be upon general-purpose skills that seemed
> to form the 'tools of the trade' for human learning.
>
> (Howe 1991: 43)

As Howe admits, such an emphasis clearly fails to take into
account the more recent view that much learning is context-
specific, not to mention the basic point that processes do need
to be applied to something! (Meadows 1993). Moreover, it
seems that knowledge and cognitive strategies act together in
quite complex ways. Schneider (1994) suggests three particularly
important ones:

- Knowledge can facilitate the use of particular strategies. For
  instance, if someone was given a list of local place names
  to remember, a good knowledge of the geography of the
  area might enable her or him to 'chunk' them in clusters or
  sequences, making less of a burden on her or his processing
  capacity.
- Previous knowledge can help learners to see links with new
  material so that they can apply established strategies in new
  situations. For example, even though they could never previously have seen the 'nonsense' words 'slare' and 'seck', readers
  could still apply their knowledge of English pronunciation and
  use a strategy like rote repetition if for some obscure reason
  they actually wanted to remember them.

A learner driver is totally involved in the act of driving, but an experienced driver can actually be concentrating on something else as they drive!

- A good knowledge base can also mean that learners have less need to think about appropriate strategies because they employ them automatically through their familiarity with the area or domain. This can be particularly important with complex tasks where several strategies may need to be coordinated (Pressley and Van 1994). A learner driver is totally involved in the act of driving but an experienced driver behaves very differently, especially on a familiar road. They do not have to size up each bend as they approach in order to decide how to tackle it, because they already *know* where to brake and where to change gear. Indeed, their performance may become so automatic that they are not aware of it and can even think about something else at the same time.

Available strategies

The fact that knowledge and strategies interact with each other in such ways means that it is impossible to produce a simple linear sequence showing how strategies develop in 'the normal child'. One of the major criticisms of Piaget's work was precisely that, in real life, children's thinking is very much affected by the content and context of the problem (Donaldson 1978). However, it is possible to outline general tendencies in the availability of different strategies, while acknowledging that their application in practice will be very uneven and far from linear in development.

- To begin with, young children seem to have very few strategies of any sort available to them. Faced by many problems, they simply do not know what to do. Thus, almost any sort of strategy instruction will help, provided of course they can put it into practice. (For a review of some of this research, see McShane 1991.)
- The earliest spontaneous strategies begin to appear when children recognize intuitively the value of prolonging the information presented to them, so that it is not lost from short-term memory. In general, rote repetition or rehearsal is the first conscious major strategy to emerge, but it represents only a shallow level of processing because the input is only repeated, not actively processed in any way.
- 'Chunking', involving both the new material and the learner's previous knowledge, represents an important development because now the stimulus is actually transformed into bigger and more meaningful chunks or units. Unlike pure rote, the actual chunks formed may differ between individuals because the new material is being related to individual preferences or to what is already known.
- Pure chunking simply involves rearranging the information, but it can be processed further by transforming it into another modality. Typically, for example, most people form visual images for verbal material they read or hear, or conversely use verbal labels to help them to deal with visual information such as a picture. The use of these transformations will be affected not only by prior knowledge but also by the strengths of the different intelligences an individual possesses or by the modalities they prefer.

- Finally, successful learners discover ways not only of transforming information, but of enriching it or elaborating on it to
  make it more meaningful or memorable, even though this
  may apparently go against common sense by adding to the
  amount to be learned. Mnemonics are a good example of this
  technique, and an often-quoted example has helped many
  children to remember the awkward sequence of letters at the
  beginning of the word 'beautiful'. The mnemonic 'Big Elephants
  Aren't Ugly, they're beautiful' provides a sequence of words
  beginning with appropriate letters. Like many mnemonics, it
  seems faintly ridiculous and hardly worth the effort, but it
  can be very effective.

These trends in the availability of strategies can also be seen
in relation to the very general shift in conceptual development
proposed in the various top-down theories of child development. The link with Vygotsky is probably the clearest. Thus rote
repetition is based entirely on the external stimulus or materials
presented, while chunking involves some internal reorganization.
Transforming requires more input from the child, and elaborative
strategies rely very heavily on what is already known. The more
cognitive effort the learner puts in, the better the material will be
learned – a fact sadly true of life in general!

Metacognition – the use and monitoring of learning strategies

This developmental trend in the availability of a range of strategies
is therefore related to the child's increasing personal involvement
in the strategies they use, and, since it is clearly not enough just
to have strategies available, the final part of this section will look
at how this metacognitive control develops. As Resnick says:

> Thinking well requires more than knowing a selected set of
> strategies or techniques for problem solving and learning. It
> also requires knowing when these strategies are appropri-
> ate, and it requires the motivation to apply them, even though
> they may involve more effort than routine performances.
>
> (Resnick 1987: 48)

In Western society at least, an all-pervading aim of child-
centred education has always been to encourage children to learn
for themselves. A particularly important reason why children's

control of their own strategies is vital is that, without such control, they are unlikely to be able to make proper use of different
techniques as independent learners. In general, studies in which
children are given instructions to use particular strategies in
specific situations or with specific sorts of materials have reported
successful results, but there have been far fewer studies demonstrating successful spontaneous use of previously taught strategies (Levin 1993). This lack of spontaneous use applies both to
the *maintenance* of a strategy in a familiar context, and even more
so to the *transfer* of a strategy to a different context. In other words,
children can often be taught to use a strategy when instructed,
but will not necessarily make it their own. Like taking a horse to
the water, you can take a child to the strategy but you cannot
make him think!

One likely explanation for this is that children may accept the
teacher's or experimenter's instructions at the time, but need to
be convinced that the strategy really does work. McShane (1991)
thus contrasts experiments in which spontaneous transfer did
and did not take place, and notes that it was much more likely
to occur if children were given feedback about the effectiveness
of the strategy. Indeed, it may be important for the learner to
conduct some sort of informal 'cost-benefit analysis' to decide
whether the challenge presented by a learning task is worth the
effort likely to be involved, and they may sometimes decide quite
rightly that it is not (Claxton *et al.* 1996).

In sum, therefore, merely having a range of strategies available
is not enough to guarantee successful learning. The child also
needs to have positive attitudes and a range of metacognitive
skills which involve an awareness of their own thinking. These
will include the ability to:

- understand the way the various strategies work and relate
  them to the demands of the task in order to select the best
  one – in other words know *when* to use a particular strategy;
- believe that the selected strategy really will help, or at least
  have the confidence and motivation to try it – in other words
  know *why* to use a particular strategy;
- be able to monitor and evaluate its use – in other words know
  how to use a particular strategy.

The child's ability to monitor and control their own use of strategies thus interacts in various ways with a range of other factors

including their existing available strategies, their knowledge of the world, their perceptions of the new strategy and their expectations of success or failure.

How changes occur

In the past, most psychologists have tended to concentrate on charting and analysing developmental changes, rather than on studying exactly how such changes might occur, perhaps because the latter is not so much open to direct observation (Simon and Halford 1995). Four approaches will be very briefly considered here:

- Computer models.
- Mismatches and development.
- Representational redescription.
- Connectionist theory.

Computer models

The enormously rapid increase in the power and speed of computers has opened up a new field of research where attempts are made to write complex programs which simulate children's cognitive development. Basically, if a program can mimic the ways in which children tackle problems in real life – including their mistakes and misconceptions – then it seems reasonable that the program is actually reflecting the way children's thinking develops. Psychologists like Rutkowska (1993) are trying to combine the approaches of artificial intelligence and cognitive psychology to improve their understanding of child development.

Caution is necessary, however, because in many ways, human beings appear to think in ways which are very different from the ways in which digital computers currently work. This is partly why computers are so useful, of course – if humans too had enormous, accurate, rapid memories, they would not need to have developed computers in the ways they have. For example, much human thinking seems to be characterized by illogical hunches and inexplicable insights rather than by logical high-speed analysis of vast amounts of stored data (Sotto 1994). On the other hand, as computer models become even more powerful and flexible, it is likely that they will be increasingly able to reflect human thinking.

Mismatches and development

Most psychological theories about how cognitive development actually occurs do seem to share a basic idea – the notion of some sort of cognitive dissonance or mismatch between what the child observes and their current understanding. This idea seems logical, and is clearly at the root of Piaget's theories (though there may be problems with any theory which proposes a series of qualitatively distinct stages because it is hard to explain exactly how the child moves on from one stage to the next). For Piaget, a concept is built up and confirmed through the 'assimilation' of further examples, but if the concept is in some way inadequate, there will come a time when it will need to change or 'accommodate' to fit a growing body of conflicting evidence.

For instance, Aliya in Cameo 2 believes that no metal things can float and can carry on believing that, assimilating further examples of non-metal things that float and metal ones that do not. She will need to modify that belief only when she recognizes conflicting evidence from her own past (such as her trip across the Channel) or when her predictions fail (as with the foil). Even then, she may prefer to maintain her concept and to seek other explanations for the discrepancy, and it is difficult to change well-established ideas which seem to have worked well in the past. Indeed, much of child-centred education can be seen not as telling children the right answer, but as putting them in situations where they will notice such incongruities and be able to change their misconceptions for themselves. They need not just sit back and wait for incongruities to arise or be presented to them, of course, and successful learners will often actively seek out mismatches to test their own ideas. Sotto (1994) for example, describes learning as realizing we do not understand something we would like to and testing out hunches about it.

Representational redescription

However, a group of studies by Karmiloff-Smith (1992) suggests that valuable learning can in fact take place without the child having to be confronted by any kind of mismatch. From her results, Karmiloff-Smith proposes a theory with the rather awe-inspiring title 'representational redescription'. This suggests that children may initially concentrate on solving a problem in the outside world, until they reach what she calls a stage of 'behavioural mastery', where there is no mismatch at all between their ideas and their observations. They may then reflect, not on what they observe, but on these successful ideas, and try out variations to check on them or refine them, sometimes even resulting temporarily in less successful or more stereotyped behaviour.

Such regressions are difficult for more traditional theories to explain, but they have certainly been observed in children's learning. In one experiment, for example, Karmiloff-Smith found that children who had developed a successful way of recording their path through a maze actually regressed to a less successful method for a while, as if deliberately checking on their solution even though it was working perfectly well and there was no need to alter it. Such reflection clearly requires the sort of metacognitive skills mentioned earlier, so if such apparently inexplicable behaviour ever occurs in the classroom, it may be some consolation to suppose that the children are not simply being irritating, but are developing their ideas through representational redescription!

Connectionist theory

Finally, psychologists are making more use of important developments in our understanding of how the brain works, and exciting links between physiology and learning theories are beginning to be made (Halford 1993). Briefly, it appears that a stimulus causes activity across a wide range of neuro connections in the brain, on many different levels. Some connections are excited, some inhibited, with the activity occurring in parallel rather than in sequence, so that this sort of approach is sometimes called 'parallel distributed processing'. The research is relatively new, and teachers might as yet be forgiven for wondering what the classroom implications might be, but it could certainly change the way we look at complex behaviour such as reading. If children really can process information at different levels at the same time, then it may not be the case that phonic and word-recognition skills *must* come before comprehension, or vice versa, but that they interact with each other in ways that psychologists are only just beginning to understand. If so, then debates about whether it is more important to begin with bottom-up or top-down approaches could become largely irrelevant, much to the relief of many primary teachers. (For a detailed review of how connectionist theory may relate for example to the development of language, categorization or drawing, see Lee and Das Gupta 1995.)

The context

Following the overview of cognitive processes presented in the previous chapter, this chapter has so far concentrated on how these processes develop. It has looked very briefly at a basic similarity between some 'big theories' of child development, then considered capacity, knowledge, available strategies and strategy control as four candidates for what actually develops, before finally suggesting some ways in which development might actually take place. Several particular implications for teachers have already been mentioned, but the final part of this chapter briefly considers in general terms some of the implications, not simply acknowledging how children think as in the previous chapter, but trying to move their thinking on in the context of the classroom.

What are teachers aiming for?

It is first worth considering exactly what sorts of cognitive skills teachers want to develop, not just for successful school learning, but to equip children for later life in society. Resnick (1987) offers a list of 'higher-order thinking skills' which is often referred to by other Western educationalists. Such thinking tends to:

- be non-algorithmic (that is, the path to the solution is not completely clear in advance and the learner cannot simply follow a series of known steps);
- be complex, involving for example different points of view;
- have several possible solutions, each with advantages and disadvantages to be weighed up;
- involve nuances of judgement and interpretation;
- depend on multiple criteria for making decisions;
- involve uncertainty because not all the necessary information is available in advance;

- depend on self-regulation rather than on instructions from someone else;
- involve imposing meaning and structure;
- involve considerable mental effort.

Significantly, Resnick herself notes that an emphasis in schools on getting the right answer in order to achieve high grades actually discourages such higher-order thinking. In a wider sense, as Chapter 5 will show, the values promoted by schools will depend on more general social values – independent, assertive thinking, for example, may well be valued in one society but shunned in another. In this respect, it is worth asking how far such apparently valuable thinking skills are reflected in the content of the National Curriculum, and there are certainly those who feel that, in order to maintain their self-determination and teach children about things that really matter, teachers may have to appropriate or even resist some of the official demands being made on them (Woods 1995). Bearing this in mind, this chapter will now consider what teachers might try to do in order to move children's thinking on to higher levels.

Behavioural approaches

Traditionally (and certainly in books on the psychology of education), there have been two supposedly conflicting approaches to developing children's learning – child-centred and behavioural, though in practice most teachers probably use a mixture of both. However, because of the tradition of child-centred primary education in this country, and because of the rather emotive terms used, it is again important to avoid setting up a dichotomy in which 'bad' behavioural methods are seen as totally opposed to 'good' child-centred ones.

Chapter 1 showed how behavioural competences, though limited, offer one approach, and there are several other sets of techniques which can also trace their origins back to behavioural psychology, including 'precision teaching' and 'direct instruction' or 'direct teaching'. Such techniques involve clearly-specified objectives defined in terms of observable behaviour, sets of very small steps for the child to work through with little chance of failure, and lots of positive feedback and reinforcement. In some cases, the programme, though constructed by the teacher, is supposed to be flexible, as in the case of precision teaching (Kessissoglou and Farrell, 1996), but in many cases the steps are fixed, to the extent that in the Distar programmes (SRA 1984) the teacher actually works through a script. Kyriacou (1995) concludes that such approaches can be very efficient in transmitting fixed bodies of knowledge, but tend not to develop creativity or deeper understanding. Moreover, they are clearly at odds with the higher-order thinking skills mentioned above because they tend to emphasize what children can *do* rather than what they *understand* (Sotto 1994).

On the other hand, as already emphasized, there is clearly also a place for knowledge in the sense of factual information, much of which is arbitrary and cannot be worked out using thinking skills alone. For example, a learner's knowledge of the world might enable them to have some idea of how Roman roads must have transformed communications in Britain, but it does not enable them to predict the Roman names of the towns they connected if they do not already know them. If a child wants to know the Roman names for various British towns, they can certainly use higher-order thinking skills or research skills to find out, and may pick up valuable techniques on the way, but ultimately someone or something, be it a teacher, another child, a map or a text, will have to provide the answer for them. If the curriculum only requires them to know the names, the temptation is to save time by simply telling them in the first place. In such cases, the objective could perhaps be summed up in a statement of competence, and a behavioural programme might be appropriate.

Strategy teaching

Other approaches have tried to acknowledge the need for the teacher to be able to observe and monitor children's progress on the one hand, and the importance of the child's own unobservable learning processes and strategies on the other. This chapter has already shown that, although strategy teaching can be very effective in the short term, children will often not improve their spontaneous use of strategies or generalize to other situations. So what can we do to improve matters?

Ashman and Conway (1993) describe several attempts to develop children's use of strategies, not simply by giving instruction in their use, but also by encouraging children to take them on for themselves. The SPELT (Strategies Program for Effective Learning and Thinking) programme, for example, consists of three main steps:

- The teacher teaches children a strategy. Examples include the use of flow charts, or listing 'positive, negative and interesting' factors when faced by a problem.
- The teacher shows the children how to use the same strategy in other situations, actually teaching them to generalize and adapt it.
- The children are encouraged to practise the strategy, adapting it for themselves.

Although this approach uses strategies provided by the teacher and is teacher-led in the early stages, there is a real attempt to get children to take on the strategies for themselves and to avoid the whole thing becoming just another form of 'right answer' exercise carried out to please the teacher and therefore acting against the development of higher-order thinking skills.

There are several other points to consider in trying to encourage more effective strategies. For example:

- Is the new strategy totally unfamiliar, or can it be compared to a method already used by the child? Does the child perceive the offered strategy as rather complex and therefore likely to involve a great deal of mental effort? (Morris 1991). Teaching a complicated mnemonic to a child who spontaneously uses only rote repetition could prove particularly difficult, and it might be better to develop the use of simpler chunking and transformational strategies first.
- Do the materials or end result seem important to the child? Lists of 'nonsense' syllables or arbitrary pairings of words or pictures may give valuable control in experimental settings, but if they seem irrelevant to the child, there is less chance of taught strategies being used again later. Likely spontaneous use of strategies thus interacts with the child's wider beliefs and knowledge of the world (David and Palincsar 1994).
- Similarly, does the strategy *look* convincing? For instance, because mnemonics involve the learning of additional, often bizarre material, they may appear at first sight to be ineffective and may therefore be rejected as not worth considering. As we saw earlier, it seems important initially to demonstrate to

the child that the strategy really is effective and ultimately for the child to be able to monitor such feedback for themselves.
- The child's past success with learning strategies is also likely to be important. As we shall see in Chapter 4, attitudes and cognitive skills interact in complex ways: a learner who expects to fail may see little point in investing a lot of effort in any strategy, particularly an unproven and potentially threatening one. This relationship is also a two-way one, so that, for example, successful spontaneous use carries with it positive attitudes like feelings of involvement in and responsibility for your own learning (Galloway and Edwards 1991).

Conclusion: teacher intervention

There are those who feel that almost any sort of teacher instruction will actually discourage real learning. A particular influence here has been Piaget, who was interested in how rational thought develops in children and was not really concerned about how adults could best intervene in the process. His work seemed to imply that if a child was not cognitively ready to learn something, there was no point trying to teach it anyway, and in the past his ideas were sometimes interpreted as meaning that teachers should wait until the necessary state of 'readiness' had been reached. Other writers such as Holt (1991) claim that learning is not the product of teaching and that the really important thing is for children to be left to 'figure things out' for themselves, with the teacher on hand only to help out at the child's request. This may currently seem an attractive proposition to over-worked teachers, but is simply unrealistic in the face of present-day public accountability.

Moving on

In philosophical terms, these two extreme positions can be traced back to a rationalist emphasis on public knowledge on the one hand and an existentialist emphasis on private self-awareness on the other. Bonnett (1994) discusses how the two can be combined into 'authentic-rational' thinking which acknowledges the importance of both. For example, teacher assessment is necessary, but should ideally be meaningful to the learner and should reflect the ways in which what they have learned has affected their ways of dealing with real problems. In a sense, combining these two aspects of learning means that the teacher becomes a mediator between the child's private understandings and the public demands of the curriculum. This theme will be taken up again in the Chapter 6, but cognitive development cannot be studied in isolation. Two other very important factors in successful teaching and learning must be considered – the attitudes of teachers and learners, and the social contexts in which they operate. These factors are considered in the next two chapters.

4

Success, attitudes and the obsessive margin drawer

Cameo 1

Ms A. has given her Year 6 children a word search and, to reinforce the word 'diagonal' which they have just met, has put one of the words in diagonally, telling them only that one of the words is written in a different way. The other words are easy to spot, and both Shane and Claire have found them. However, Claire has declared that 'this is boring' and is chatting loudly and openly to her friend, while Shane, sitting next to her, is still trying. When Ms A. goes over, Claire asks her to tell them where the word is, but Shane begs her not to.

Cameo 2

Joanne is a student teacher with lots of previous experience with children, who is doing particularly well on teaching practice. However, her own lesson evaluations and discussions with her teacher and her tutor are very negative, in spite of their frequent encouragement and praise. A lively response from the children is seen as a loss of control, and the slightest hitch turns a lesson into 'a total disaster' as far as Joanne is concerned.

Cameo 3

Tony has been set some writing to do. What he actually does is:

1 Appears to search for a ruler, which is actually plainly visible in his drawer, and chats with other children while doing so (2 minutes).

2 Returns to his seat, then goes back and searches for a pencil in same way (2 minutes).

3 Joins back of queue to use pencil sharpener on the teacher's desk, politely letting others come in front of him (2 minutes).

4 Breaks point of pencil by deliberately pressing very hard, so that he has to sharpen it again (another 2 minutes).

5 Repeats step 4.

6 Hides pencil under paper, then accuses neighbour of stealing it (2 minutes).

7 Finally draws margin very carefully and very heavily, then immediately decides that it is 3mm too far to the left and needs to be rubbed out (30 seconds).

8 Starts squabble with neighbour about use of their rubber (2 minutes).

9 Repeats steps 7 and 8, drawing heavily so that it takes longer to rub out.

10 Having finally drawn the margin, helpfully volunteers to collect in everybody's work, as it is now the end of the session!

The teacher

The happiest days of your life?

What was your own worst subject at school? Pause for a moment, grit your teeth and think about it. For example:

- How did you *feel* just before that lesson and then during it?
- How did you get on with the teacher?
- Did you have any ways of trying to avoid the work or showing how weak you were at it?
- How did you feel about pupils who were good at that subject?
- Can you say exactly what it was that made it your worst subject?
- Were there any activities that you particularly disliked, or any that weren't quite so bad?
- Has it had any effect on your life? How do you feel about this subject now?

Generally speaking, most teachers or others involved in education did quite well in most subjects when they were at school, and feel positive about education to the extent that they have wanted to go back and inflict it on other people! It can therefore be hard to imagine what school must be like for children who consistently experience failure, but it may be helpful for teachers to think back to how they felt about any failure they themselves experienced, especially if they can also compare notes with a partner or friend, where their different perceptions may be quite revealing. This chapter is very much about the relationships between success and failure on the one hand, and attitudes and feelings on the other.

Defending the self against failure

In any situation that makes people feel that they have failed, they can generally react in one of two ways. They can either accept that they have failed, and risk feeling guilty about it, or they can in some way reject the situation, or at least try to avoid it. In remembering their worst subject, many adults will recall rejecting the work and being disruptive, or using some of the classic work avoidance strategies, such as obsessive pencil sharpening – which we will discuss later in this chapter – but they may also have reacted in less obvious ways, especially if they generally worked successfully in most other subjects. Particularly if people think they *ought* to be able to do better, failure makes them feel guilty.

So how do people defend themselves against such unpleasant feelings? Psychologists interested in this area often take a 'psychodynamic' approach which suggests that many deep feelings can be traced back to experiences in early childhood which have since been forgotten or repressed. The name of Sigmund Freud is commonly associated with such ideas, but it is possible to gain valuable insights about our own and our children's feelings without necessarily studying psychodynamic theory in detail, and there's no need to lie on a couch while reading the rest of this chapter! For a very practical summary of the psychodynamic and other approaches to children's behaviour, see Ayers *et al.* (1995).

One particular area of psychodynamic theory which does offer such insights is the notion of 'defence mechanisms' and some of them have entered everyday language. Some of the best-known ones are outlined briefly below, and in each case an example is first offered which could relate to normal adult experience, in order to help understanding of similar reactions in children.

Regression

As the term implies, this means going back to an earlier situation or stage of development where a current problem either did not exist, or where there was no expectation that it could be solved. Most adults will admit that they have occasionally resorted to sulks, tears or temper tantrums, and letting feelings out in childish ways may actually help occasionally.

In children, regression often appears as immature behaviour from a child who can act in more mature ways under different circumstances. In a way, the emotional aspects of the behaviour which will be discussed later as 'learned helplessness' involve going back to a stage where the child is more like a helpless infant from whom nothing can be expected. In extreme forms, a child may start to wet the bed because of feeling threatened by the birth of a new baby in the family, demonstrating that they too need the attention being lavished on the new arrival.

Rationalization

This is also generally well known, and is particularly popular with fluent, thoughtful adults such as teachers! It involves thinking up an acceptable reason for failure or bad behaviour, allowing the real, less acceptable reason to be repressed. A teacher may decide at the last minute to let the children draw a picture, 'to develop their eye-motor coordination', when the real reason for doing so is in fact that he or she left it too late to plan anything! Or, they may give their class only very basic, non-stretching work to do on a display, such as drawing round stencils or sticking on hundreds of bits of screwed up tissue paper. If they then spend several hours after school working on the more creative parts of the display themselves, they may claim to be doing this because the children are not capable of it, but the real reason could be that they want their display to look better than Mr Michaelangelo's next door.

Although they may be less good at it, children too may come up with amazing explanations, such as complicated excuses for having forgotten their PE kit for the fifth week in succession, when all they really want to do is avoid PE. This can even form the basis for an English activity with older children, where they have to think up bizarre explanations for having jam all over their faces while carrying five left-foot wellington boots!

Projection

This involves literally 'projecting' unacceptable behaviour or attitudes on to others. If someone feels uncomfortable about their own aggressive impulses, one way of avoiding the unpleasant emotions is to convince themselves that other people are behaving threateningly towards them, so that their own aggression is perfectly understandable. This is neatly summed up by the well-known motto 'retaliate first!' Similarly, when people look back to their worst subject, it is quite likely that they disliked the teacher and felt that the teacher disliked them. They can therefore blame their lack of success on the appalling personality, unfair treatment or professional shortcomings of the teacher.

Reaction formation

If someone has feelings which are threatening or in some way unacceptable, they may repress them by acting in the very opposite way from the way they really feel. For example, most teachers feel that they are not supposed to have favourites or to heartily dislike any of their pupils, yet as human beings it is almost impossible not to like some children more than others. I can certainly remember taking an almost instant dislike to one boy, who appeared very sly and surly. This must have caused guilt feelings because, almost without realizing it, I found myself being particularly nice to him and it was significant that by Christmas, I had *almost* genuinely got to like him! Conversely, of course, teachers sometimes realize that they are developing 'favourites' who are in danger of becoming resented by the rest of the class, and may thus come publicly to expect higher standards of work or behaviour from them than from the rest, quickly expressing annoyance or disappointment when they fail to reach these higher standards.

Children may find it harder to react in ways which are the opposite of how they feel, though peer pressure can certainly result in a child showing great enthusiasm for something which secretly they do not really like.

Displacement

If a teacher feels unfairly criticized by their Head, they may feel unable to shout back, or to set fire to the Head's executive swivel chair, which is what they would really like to do. Instead, they may well take it out on their class that afternoon, or wait until they go home and criticize their partner, kick the cat and slam all the doors! Displacement can thus be about finding a safe target, and bullying can be seen as one particularly disturbing form of displacement activity. Here a child who feels frustrated may be unable to vent their anger on the teacher or parent whom they see as responsible for their frustration, and so will pick on a weaker child instead.

Work-avoidance could be seen as another type of displacement, in which children try to avoid doing something unpleasant or threatening by doing something pleasant or unthreatening instead. A child who feels anxious about their work can, if a real expert at displacement, spend nearly 20 minutes drawing the margin, as we saw in Cameo 3! Adults may feel that they are above such petty devices, but I will admit that, faced with the increasingly urgent need to write this chapter, I found many jobs around the house that suddenly needed doing, then felt that a break and a cup of coffee were deserved, even before a single word had actually been written!

Fantasizing

This may not always appear on lists of defence mechanisms, but it clearly serves the same purpose. Fantasies are always more attractive than the situations in which people find themselves when they indulge in them, and they provide a temporary escape. Better still, we can actually overcome problems through fantasies, defeating the awkward parent with a crushing rejoinder or even a well-placed karate chop, or earning the Head's unstinting admiration and eternal gratitude by our brilliant teaching, breathtaking displays or perfect policy documents.

Children too may indulge in fantasies, and it is often obvious to teachers that they are 'miles away', lost in a daydream. Some of this may simply be due to the limited span of attention, and therefore not be a cause for undue concern. Sometimes they may share their fantasies with adults, and young children may often seem unable to distinguish between reality and fantasy. But fantasizing can become a real defence mechanism for some children, particularly if they feel unwanted – they may for instance claim to be about to receive wonderful presents or be taken on luxurious holidays. It may be kinder, at least in the short term, for teachers to make envious noises rather than to call their bluff, though in the long term such children need to feel valued for the person they really are rather than the person they would like to be.

Sublimation and compensation

It may seem that most of the defence mechanisms so far are not in fact solutions at all, since they merely enable people's true feelings to be hidden and at the most only avoid the problem for a while. However, some defence mechanisms can actually be very positive and productive. In sublimation, an unacceptable trait or desire can be channelled into an acceptable form, so that aggressive impulses may be channelled into contact sports, for example. Similarly, people may sometimes go to extreme lengths to compensate for something perceived as a weakness, and actually come to excel at it. Many famous actors claim that they were painfully shy as children, for instance, and it is not unknown for teachers to become curriculum coordinators in subjects at which they have worked very hard because they initially found them difficult.

Teachers' attitudes to children who fail

So far, this section has considered some ways in which both adults and children may try to protect themselves against unpleasant feelings such as those caused by failure. But before going on to look more closely at children's attitudes and behaviour in the classroom, it will be useful to consider teachers' own attitudes to children who are failing, since this again is something not normally done. To teachers, of course, such children are a particular cause of concern, and although the reasons may seem obvious, it is worth pausing for a moment to think exactly why this is so. There are several sorts of reason:

- For most people, part of their motivation for going into teaching is that they like children and want to be involved in the important job of helping them to learn. (At least, that's what most candidates for teacher training courses have told me over the years!) Interestingly, such attitudes are very difficult to pin down in terms of competences, to the extent that one teacher thought 'it would be possible to develop the DfEE competences to an acceptable level and yet thoroughly dislike children'! (Mahoney 1996: 148). Teachers will thus naturally be particularly concerned about children who are not learning or making the most of their potential, and this is the most common and publicly acceptable reason.

- Consequently, if some children fail to learn in spite of the teacher's efforts, the teacher may feel a sense of frustration. If he or she has tried six ways of showing a child that 3×4 is the same as 4×3 and they still do not understand, the teacher may have an uncomfortable sense of failure which will encourage them to blame the child's lack of ability or effort rather than their own teaching, or to summon up other defence mechanisms. Even if the child has tried really hard, the teacher may still have these negative feelings which should be recognized.

- The child may not have tried hard, of course. Many children who are failing also protect themselves from failure by refusing to work or by being openly disruptive. Most teachers are obviously also concerned about the threat that this presents to their authority, though a few may find it hard to admit, especially in schools where such admissions are discouraged or seen as a sign of incompetence. Such children can therefore sometimes be seen as a potential threat to the teacher's position which cannot be shared.

- Not all unsuccessful children disrupt, of course. Some protect themselves by withdrawing and giving up before they start, thus rejecting the teacher's efforts just as much as the disruptive children do. Such rejection is very hard not to take personally, especially if the teacher has invested a lot of time and effort in the activity, and there is a sense in which a failing child implies that the teacher too has failed. Because this may represent an even deeper, personal threat rather than just a professional one, it can become a cause for resentment yet remain hard to recognize.

Bearing these different feelings in mind, this section ends by noting the ways in which teachers tend to relate children's attitudes to their success or lack of it. Most teachers will have felt threatened or rejected by children's lack of interest in their wonderful activities, and will have blamed the children's subsequent failure on their poor attitudes. 'If you'd listened, you'd have known what to do!' or 'You won't find the answer by looking out of the window!' or simply 'Stop talking and get on with your work!'

Understandably, teachers see children's failure as a *result* of negative attitudes, but a major theme of this chapter is that it is a two-way relationship and that failure, or the expectation of it, can also be a *cause* of negative attitudes and behaviour. The next section looks at children's attitudes and how they relate to achievement, while the final section considers how teachers can encourage more positive classroom attitudes and the success that accompanies them.

The child

Children's theories about intelligence

Whether they are aware of them or not, everybody has implicit theories about most things that are important to them, including their own and children's learning. If a teacher comments on a child's home background or alters their plans for the afternoon because of the dreaded wet-weather dinner time, they are implying some general beliefs about factors which they think affect children's learning. Children too have these implicit theories and a particularly important one which is strongly related to their attitudes to school work is to do with their beliefs about the nature of intelligence. Dweck (1989) suggests that many children have one of two intuitive theories of intelligence:

- *Entity theory* which sees intelligence as fixed and unchangeable. Such children prefer tasks where they can perform well in relation to others and thus demonstrate a high level of ability, or at least avoid looking stupid.
- *Incremental theory* which sees intelligence as able to be developed. Such children prefer tasks which allow them to improve their skills, even if they are not successful at first.

If there are in fact several different sorts of intelligence, as discussed in Chapter 2, it will be possible for learners to have
different ideas about their abilities in different subject areas, and
thus to prefer different sorts of tasks in each.

In fact, these beliefs and preferences are tied in with a whole
cluster of attitudes which tend to distinguish between successful
and unsuccessful learners, particularly in their attitudes to failure
or challenge. Stevenson and Palmer (1994) present a useful summary of these, and Dweck and her colleagues have carried out a
number of interesting studies in this area (see Dweck 1989 for a
review). In a typical experiment, children were presented with
some problems which they could all do, followed by some which
were too difficult for them. Even when faced with exactly the same
experience of success followed by failure, the children tended to
separate into two groups distinguished by their attitudes to this
identical experience. These attitudes tend to be generally typical
of many successful or unsuccessful learners, as briefly illustrated
in the behaviour of Claire and Shane in Cameo 1.

Mastery orientation and learned helplessness

Successful learners tend to show 'mastery orientation' – a certain
set of positive attitudes which allow them to see lack of immediate success as a challenge rather than a failure. They tend to
give themselves subvocal instructions, and stay on task because
they believe that they will eventually solve the problem. They
tend not to be interested in easy tasks which do not allow them
to demonstrate their ability to learn, and relish the effort needed
to succeed at difficult but achievable tasks.

In contrast, many unsuccessful learners exhibit a set of negative attitudes about themselves and the task, sometimes referred
to as 'learned helplessness'. They see lack of immediate success
as evidence of their low, fixed ability, and reject challenging tasks,
perhaps claiming that they are boring. They try to avoid potential failure either directly, or through the distraction of claiming
to have other skills or successes. They tend to choose easy tasks,
or occasionally impossibly difficult ones which they cannot be
blamed for failing, and see tasks that require a lot of effort as
demonstrating their lack of ability.

It will be clear that the attitudes displayed in mastery orientation are closely related to the sorts of learning teachers wish to

encourage, and are far more than a by-product. For example, Resnick's (1987) 'higher order thinking skills' (Chapter 2) involve accepting uncertainty and mental effort, both of which are incompatible with learned helplessness. It will therefore be helpful to look more closely at these sets of attitudes and their effects on classroom learning (see also Fisher 1995).

Eisner and Seligman (1994) analyze children's and adults' 'explanatory styles' further, showing how they can result in either the pessimistic style displayed by learned helplessness, or an optimistic style reflected in mastery orientation. They propose three dimensions which distinguish between the two sets of attitudes to failure, and these are briefly discussed below.

Stable/unstable causes of failure

Children who attribute failure to a stable cause such as low ability or consistently being unlucky will expect to fail in the future and will see little point in trying. Those who see the failure as the result of an unstable cause such as a headache can argue that they may have failed on this particular problem, but they may do better or be luckier next time.

Global/specific causes of failure

If they see the causes as being global, or affecting many areas of their life, children will experience widespread and damaging learned helplessness. If you think back to your own worst subject, your negative feelings about it are likely to be restricted just to that subject or one or two others, rather than to everything you did at school. You were probably able to see yourself as being no good at that subject, rather than useless at everything.

Internal/external locus of control

Children displaying learned helplessness tend to attribute failure to external locus of control – that is to a cause outside themselves, such as fate or the arbitrary whims of their teacher, so that there is little they can do about failing. In contrast, successful learners tend to show internal locus of control and to feel responsible for their own results.

Self-esteem and attitudes to the self

It will be obvious from the above that many unsuccessful learners have negative attitudes, not only about tasks which are likely to pose the threat of failure, but also about themselves as learners. The literature on the self is often complex, and forms an important part of a humanistic approach to psychology which differs in some respects from the general emphasis on more cognitive approaches in this book. It is not the intention to go into any great detail here, but for a good summary see, for example, Helmke (1994).

It is however helpful to summarize some of the main terms relating to the self:

- *Self-concept* – the sort of person we think we are in general, including our self-image.
- *Self-image* – the image we have of our own bodies as well as of our personalities, our various skills and attributes.
- *Ideal self* – the sort of person each of us would ideally like to be.
- *Possible selves* – our visions of the various people we think we could become. These can be both positive (such as the rich self or the self as expert in some area) or negative (for example the self as a teacher failed by the inspectors).
- *True self* – the sort of person we really are, though this may be very hard to discover!
- *Self-esteem* – how we value ourselves. Self-esteem will be low if there is a wide gap between self-image and ideal self. This is obviously a crucial factor with major effects on learning, and a great deal has been written about raising children's self-esteem in order to improve their learning (see Gurney 1988; Lawrence 1996).

However, one or two other points should be remembered when the importance of self-esteem in the classroom is considered.

Self-esteem and success

A high level of self-esteem gives children the confidence to explore new environments and take on challenges, and it does seem obvious that a child with high self-esteem will be a more successful learner than one with low self-esteem. But the relationship between them is a two-way one, so that improved self-esteem

A high level of self-esteem gives children the confidence to explore new environments

can be both a cause and a result of improved learning (Marsh 1990). Thus, many teachers of emotionally disturbed children, who tend to have particularly low self-esteem, concentrate on improving academic work as an effective way of making children feel better about themselves. Wilce (1994) refers to research suggesting that programmes designed to develop academic skills actually produce higher self-esteem than programmes explicitly designed to enhance it.

Self-esteem and culture

The cultural context in which self-esteem is developed and expressed is also important, and is a theme taken up in the next chapter. In Western society generally, self-reliance and individuality are valued and, at least to some extent, are encouraged in school, while in other cultures, too high a level of self-esteem may be regarded as antisocial. Wilce (1994) also concludes that many American children have very high self-esteem whether it is justified or not!

Self-esteem and reality

Self-esteem also needs to be based on a realistic self-concept or true self. Most teachers have probably come across those highly irritating children who, usually encouraged by doting parents, regard themselves as geniuses who do not need to bother with the mundane and patronizing work we give them. The temptation is to deflate them by setting fiendishly difficult tasks, but such attitudes could be one form of defence mechanism.

Self-esteem and communication

Similarly, teachers cannot always rely on what children say about themselves as giving an accurate picture of how they really feel, since it takes them many years to learn to be aware of, identify and communicate their feelings (Meadows 1993). Both adults and children may also deliberately disguise their feelings about them-selves. This can be cultural, based on embarrassment about 'blow-ing your own trumpet'. For instance, many teachers seem to find it harder to share their successes than to be self-critical about their failures.

This seemed the problem with Joanne in Cameo 2, where her tutor and teacher were concerned that she had very low self-esteem, as up to a point she really did. Eventually, however, they realized that she had learned to enjoy all the 'strokes' of praise and encouragement, and had become what Holt (1991) calls a 'praise junkie'. As a result, when others provided *less* praise, she quickly became much more positive about herself!

This section has looked at some factors which affect learners' attitudes towards themselves and towards learning in general. Bearing these in mind, we can now consider how such attitudes tend to manifest themselves in the context of the classroom.

The context

Classroom responses to failure

The first section of this chapter emphasized teachers' attitudes to failure and the second offered an analysis of children's attitudes. It is now time to look at how these attitudes are manifested in classroom behaviour, before considering how teachers can help promote more positive attitudes and the success that accompanies them. This final section begins by asking what sorts of attitude and behaviour teachers would ideally *like* to see when children cannot immediately solve a problem.

Responses to failure – what do teachers want?

If most teachers were to make a list, it might well include responses such as:

- not giving up immediately because their first attempt fails, but simply stopping to think about the problem, perhaps trying out some other ideas to see if they work;
- discussing it with another child, but not just copying the other child's work;
- considering where they could find the answer for themselves – for instance in a dictionary or reference book, or on part of a display;
- trying to see if this problem is similar to a previous one or to something they *do* understand;
- leaving the problem temporarily and working on something else in the meantime;
- having tried at least some of the above, asking the teacher for help.

All these are responses associated with successful learning, and some teachers discuss them with children and try to get them to use such strategies. Some classrooms, for example, have a list like the one above actually posted on the wall, and children know they are expected to try at least one strategy before asking the teacher for help. A similar idea is a poster making it clear what is acceptable and what is not, such as this one for maths, produced by some Tower Hamlets teachers:

> Working together isn't CHEATING
> Using a calculator isn't CHEATING
> Finding out the answer from the back of the book and trying
>   to work out how they got it isn't CHEATING
> CHEATING is pretending you understand when you don't.
> That's when you're CHEATING yourself.
>   (Access Department, Bethnal Green Centre 1987)

Such behaviour is strongly related to mastery orientation because even where the child asks for help, the emphasis is on achieving success by their own efforts as far as possible.

Now consider, in contrast, how lots of children actually behave in practice when faced with something they cannot do, and what such behaviour reveals about their attitudes.

Responses to failure – what do teachers get?

Defence mechanisms

For a start, teachers may sometimes be able to recognize when children are using some of the defence mechanisms discussed earlier. They may regress to more infantile and helpless forms of behaviour, or vent their frustration on a weaker child rather than on the teacher. But there are several other more direct ways of avoiding failure.

Impulsivity: get it over with

Some children may produce one answer very quickly, even though a little thought would show them that it is obviously not right. Such impulsive behaviour usually implies an attitude where the child wants to get the unpleasant situation over as quickly as possible. Once they have come up with an answer, no matter how inappropriate, responsibility for what happens next is shifted on to the teacher as the external 'locus of control' and they can become helpless again. On a different level, a child reading aloud may look only at the first letter or two of a difficult word and immediately come up with a totally inappropriate response, or even something that is not a word at all.

Work avoidance 1: stick to the easy bits

Children may also try to avoid something difficult by concentrating on aspects of the task which are not threatening. For example, given some writing and drawing to do, many children will always draw the picture first and take as long as possible over doing so. If they are real experts at work avoidance tactics, they can easily spend nearly twenty minutes on 'displacement' activities like drawing a margin, while claiming to be on task the whole time, as Tony did in Cameo 3 at the beginning of this chapter.

Work avoidance 2: have a wander round

If no aspects of the task appeal to them, children may get away for a time with just wandering round while their harrassed teacher is involved with other children who actually want attention. This is especially effective if, like Tony, they have an instant excuse such as looking for that ruler. Even better, if they can disturb other children and stop them from working too, this makes their own lack of achievement less obvious.

Work avoidance 3: get out of it entirely!

A more extreme tactic is to try to avoid not just the difficult parts of the task or even the whole of it, but to escape from the entire situation by getting out of the room. The most obvious way is to ask to go to the toilet, but more sophisticated techniques include deliberately getting your hands or clothes dirty, then asking to go and get cleaned up, or claiming that you have been told to go and see another teacher.

Blame it on the task

Another favourite is to dismiss the task by saying, 'This is *boring*!' or 'This is *stupid*!' In doing so, children are demonstrating that any lack of success is simply a result of not trying, and is therefore due to lack of effort rather than lack of ability, in keeping with what was said earlier about the attitudes involved in learned helplessness.

Do not listen

If they do not expect to succeed, children can minimize failure even before they start by not paying attention when the teacher introduces and explains the task. If the teacher then accuses them of not listening, they may not even bother to deny it because it is better to blame failure on inattention rather than stupidity. If so, they may deliberately make their lack of attention obvious, and not even have the decency to *pretend* to be listening! As before, if they can disrupt other children's concentration too, so much the better.

Just do nothing

If the teacher realizes that a child is not working and goes over to see them, or even if the child asks for help, the battle is still not lost. Learned helplessness means that children will simply not try for themselves, relying on the teacher to keep giving them more and more help or clues, or even eventually just to tell them the answer. Children who do this may simply want attention, of course, or they may have realized that time is short and that the teacher will probably give up before they do! Failing to get through to a child, or getting no response from them, is an uncomfortable feeling for most teachers, and they may unconsciously be pressurized into taking the easy way out and either giving the answer away, or moving on to a more responsive and rewarding pupil, with a vague threat to return later.

Easy riders

Unsuccessful learners may have a range of attitudes towards gaining the teacher's attention. As has already been suggested, some will actually want to make their lack of effort obvious to avoid seeming stupid, but others will keep a low profile and try to avoid attention because they don't want their failure to be apparent. If the teacher realizes children cannot do a task, they might generate further pressure by trying to teach them! Some children may just sit there quietly doing nothing, or at least try to look busy. Others will work deliberately very slowly or will only get on when they think the teacher's attention is on them. Galton and Willcocks (1983) referred to such children as 'easy riders' and although their slow rate of work may not exactly be a response to failure, it is clearly very different from mastery orientation, and serves to keep the risk of failure to a minimum.

Cheat!

If children can delay getting on with their work by just a minute or two, and are sitting next to a successful child, they can of course resort to copying. Teachers need to be aware of the different motivations here. A lesson plan might begin with a series of impressive sounding aims and objectives such as 'to understand the legacy of settlement' or 'to recognize the number relationship between coordinates in the first quadrant of related points on a line or in a shape', both of which I have shamelessly copied from National Curriculum Programmes of Study (PoS). Copying from a neighbour will clearly not enable such grand aims to be realized. However, for various reasons, these aims may not be apparent to the children, and it is significant that, if asked, many children are unable to explain the purpose of what they are doing (Cullingford 1991). In any case, they will have quite different aims of their own. These may include producing a neat page of work which will earn a nice red tick, or not letting the teacher realize that they do not understand. In both cases, copying does achieve what the child wants.

Destroy the evidence

Finally, as something of a last resort, if they cannot avoid producing something which they know is wrong or of a poor standard, some children may resort to hiding, 'losing' or even destroying their work rather than risk having it seen by the teacher. They may pressurize other children not to produce too much work so that their own lack of success is less obvious, or, even worse, they may destroy the work of others who are likely to show them up.

Significantly, the list of undesirable responses to failure is much longer than the list of responses teachers would like! So what can be done in the face of such problems?

Promoting positive attitudes

Understanding negative responses

Such exasperating behaviour will be familiar to almost all teachers. It is also quite obvious that the first list, the behaviour teachers would like to see, reflects mastery orientation, while the responses in the second list are typical of learned helplessness. These undesirable sorts of behaviour can be understood, not only as *causes* of learning failure, but as the *results* of an underlying set of attitudes to learning, very different from the attitudes of successful learners.

Understanding why children may behave in these ways represents a first step towards doing something about it, or at least of not taking it too personally and having a nervous breakdown! Moreover, because the behaviour is a result of attitudes towards something important in the child's life, it will take a long time to do anything about it. Think for a moment of something you feel strongly about. (Capital punishment? Eating meat? Ofsted?) Would you really expect someone to be able to change your attitude completely in an hour or two?

Setting up tasks

The different attitudes involved in mastery orientation and learned helplessness mean that children who want to succeed will on the whole prefer different sorts of tasks to children who are afraid of failing. There are three factors we can consider here when setting up tasks: preferred goals, task difficulty, and attitude to effort, and bearing these factors in mind will help identify tasks which some children are likely to reject or see as threatening.

- *Preferred goals*: if children who fall back on learned helplessness tend to believe that intelligence is fixed, they will also tend to prefer tasks which demonstrate that they are reasonably intelligent, and to avoid tasks which may show them up as unintelligent. However, children who think ability can be improved by effort will prefer more challenging tasks which show them to be good learners, and which enable them to improve their skills by presenting problems to be solved. As in the Cameo 1, such children may be desperate *not* to be given the answer! The first sort of goal is therefore sometimes called a 'performance' goal because it shows what they can already do, while the second is a 'learning' goal because it shows how they can improve.
- *Task difficulty*: if children want to avoid failure, they will obviously choose tasks which are easy, but the link with task difficulty is not quite so straightforward because they may also sometimes choose impossibly difficult tasks, on the grounds that nobody can then blame them for failing. For example, some poor readers may occasionally choose a huge, difficult

library book, not only for the status it conveys but also because nobody can criticize them for failing to read it. In some cases, success itself may even be seen as a potential threat, partly because it conflicts with such children's established self-image and is thus difficult to cope with, and partly because it may raise the teacher's expectations of future success. Conversely, children who want to show their mastery of learning will prefer tasks which are reasonably difficult and challenging but which offer a good chance of achieving success eventually.

- *Attitude to effort*: for children who believe that intelligence is fixed, having to work hard at something suggests that they have low ability, which they wish to avoid. (If you have to work hard, you must be stupid!) For children who see intelligence as improvable, working at something enables them to make such improvements, and they will actually prefer tasks which require a reasonable amount of effort.

The implications for task setting, however, are not so simple – teachers can hardly tell one child that a task needs them to work at it because it is quite difficult, then turn to their neighbour and say the same task is really easy, especially if they actually expect the second child to find it harder than the first! What they might be able to do sometimes, however, is to offer the whole task as a relatively open-ended challenge to some children, and break it down into smaller units, as with a behavioural programme, for others.

Behavioural techniques

Breaking tasks down into small steps with lots of positive reinforcement does seem one way of making learning less threatening and more successful, which in turn should foster positive feelings, especially with the use of stickers or charts for children to record their progress (Merrett 1993). Such approaches can be valuable initially, but they rely on performance goals set by the teacher and may in the long run foster passive attitudes which have more in common with learned helplessness than mastery orientation. Stevenson and Palmer (1994) go a step further and review research suggesting that setting specific difficult goals can actually disrupt performance, and that a non-specific goal such as simply doing your best can be more effective, partly because it reduces anxiety.

Teacher as model

We have already seen how teachers can model cognitive skills by making their expertise more explicit and available, and the same thing obviously applies to modelling appropriate attitudes. Thus a teacher might use some form of spoken protocol to show how they cope with failure or uncertainty:

'I've made a silly mistake here. Let's go over it again and see where I went wrong,'

'I've no idea what the answer to that is, Jason. Where could I go for help?'

'I'm not sure if this is right. Let's try it out and see, and if it's wrong let's try something else.'

It is useful for teachers to recognize their own implicit theories about ability and learning (Claxton 1996) and to be careful that these theories do not cause them inadvertently to model the very attitudes they wish to discourage (Galloway and Edwards 1991). For instance, most of us have at some time described a child as 'not very bright', but such a statement implies an entity theory of intelligence, which is related to learned helplessness.

As for why teachers are tempted to describe children in such ways, they too can be seen as trying to use an entity theory to avoid failure. If the child is hopelessly lacking in ability, the teacher cannot be blamed for failing to teach them. In a sense, because teachers can thus convince themselves that there is nothing they can do, they are also learning to act in a helpless way towards a child who presents a problem. This may be an uncomfortable idea which some teachers might not accept, just as children will tend to cling to their helpless behaviour patterns and not want them to be challenged.

Specific activities

Some examples of programmes specifically designed to develop cognitive skills were discussed in Chapter 2, and from what has been said already, it will be apparent that such skills go together with positive attitudes. The motto of Feuerstein's Instrumental Enrichment programme, for example (Sharron and Coulter 1994), is 'Just a minute – let me think!' and one of the chief aims is to

English

Write about any English work you have done which you are pleased with

Writing

Reading

Speaking and listening

(a)

Figure 4.1(a) (b) As the RoA illustration shows, children can also be encouraged to recognize and come to terms with their failures!

DISASTER Areas

(b)

encourage children not to act impulsively or in other ways symptomatic of learned helplessness.

Records of achievement (RoA) represent another approach. At one level, entries in an RoA folder can chart pupils' success as they work through a programme of work and at their worst, they can become just another teacher-directed task where the whole class has to produce a piece of work in best handwriting for the RoA folder. At their best they can encourage children to think positively about themselves, to celebrate their successes and to take more responsibility for monitoring their own learning in line with what was said earlier about metacognitive skills (see Johnson *et al.* 1992 for further discussion and examples).

Moving on

Finally, children's attitudes and the ways in which they are manifest in behaviour clearly depend a lot on the social context in which they are expressed, and it would be wrong to imply that individual children's positive attitudes can be promoted in isolation. The next chapter therefore looks at these social contexts, including examples of group activities specifically designed to promote successful learning.

5

Donald Duck, Hitler and Adam and Eve: the social context of success

Cameo 1

My father was a teacher, and just about the only piece of advice he ever gave me was not to go into teaching, which is of course exactly what I did. He once told me how one of his colleagues was having a discussion with his class which included the following exchange:

Teacher: What's the first thing you think of when I say 'chips' Arthur?
Arthur: Sir, fish, sir. [They were very polite in those days].
Teacher: No! Jean?
Jean: Sir, pie?
Teacher: No! Egg, the answer's egg!

Cameo 2

It is almost the end of the day, and Mrs J. is attempting to bring her class of 5-year-olds to order by calling, 'Let's see who's ready to go home.' Most of the children immediately fold their arms uncomfortably high on their chests and sit up so straight that one or two actually achieve lift-off from their seats. As they are leaving, a few minutes later, David goes to ask Mrs J. something. As he gets close to her, he raises his hand in the air, then begins to speak.

Introduction

Social levels of learning

Teaching and learning are social activities. At one level – the macro level – this is very obviously true, with public debate and general discussion about the curriculum, finance or accountability all reflecting the cultural roles and responsibilities of education. Thus some of the questions raised in Chapter 1 were about who controls the curriculum and what our society means by a successful teacher. Social factors are equally obvious at the micro level of the school and the classroom, where learning takes place in social settings with their own peculiar rules and rituals, as illustrated in Cameo 2. A whole approach to children's learning, called the 'systems' or 'ecosystemic' approach, has been built on this idea, emphasizing that learning difficulties do not simply lie within the child but are a product of the interactions between the child and others, and the perceptions they have of each other (Ayers *et al.* 1995).

The social context is rather less obvious – but just as important – at the individual level, where learning is constantly mediated through social encounters and understandings. For instance, when I asked you Beryl's surname in Chapter 1, I broke an unwritten rule which helps define the relationship between reader and writer in a comprehension question. Similarly, even in the very individual act of reading, I break another implicit rule of social communication left to right from write to decide suddenly I if problem a you cause and.

The rest of this chapter will look at the social contexts of learning at the following three broad levels:

- The level of the culture or the community and its values.
- The settings of the school and the class.
- The ways in which individual learning is socially mediated.

As usual, discussion will be divided into three sections for convenience – the child, the teacher and the school context.

The child

Individual learning

Most of the discussion so far has taken a 'constructivist' view of children's learning – that is, a view based on the idea that children actively construct understandings by taking in information and relating it to what they already know: comparing, evaluating, predicting, making inferences and so on. However, psychologists have increasingly recognized that children do not do these things in isolation, and that social contexts, like attitudes and emotions, are not simply background factors, but have major effects on an individual's learning. Almost everything people learn is socially mediated because it involves communications from other people, whether it is picked it up in a classroom, from a book, or behind the bicycle sheds. Such views of learning thus come under the impressive-sounding title of 'social constructivism'. Similarly, when learners make decisions and act on the basis of their implicit theories about the world, these theories have in turn been developed through interactions with other people, a view which carries the even more impressive-sounding name 'symbolic interactionism'. (For a full discussion and examples, see Kutnick and Rogers 1994, or Pollard and Filer 1995).

One area of research which has become particularly popular recently concerns how children come to recognize what other people are thinking, and thus to understand their behaviour. This area, called 'theory of mind', therefore illustrates neatly some of the links between individual cognition and social awareness (Perner 1991).

Many experiments into theory of mind are based on what is called a 'false belief paradigm'. In a typical study, children of different ages watch while somebody hides a toy or sweet, then leaves the room. A second person then hides it somewhere else. The children are then asked not where the object is, but where the first person *thinks* it is, even though that belief is false and not shared by the child. This basic social situation of knowing what someone else does not know can be a very powerful and dramatic one, ranging from shouting 'Look out behind you!' at the pantomime, to the dramatic irony of King Duncan commenting on the nice friendly atmosphere at Macbeth's castle, and it is clearly something we have to learn to understand. Young children, whose thinking is still dominated by what Piaget called egocentricism, find this difficult, but most can answer correctly by the age of 5 or so (Light 1993). They can then progress to more difficult situations. For instance:

Lucy is having a video for her birthday.
It is a surprise.
Paul knows she is having a video.
Paul knows that Lucy does not know.

In order to understand the final sentence, children have to have developed 'second order' awareness of other people's thinking, and this tends to happen roughly between the ages of 6 and 9 (Leekham 1993). Now try a more difficult one:

Lucy is having a video for her birthday.
She knows about it.
Paul knows, but thinks she does not know about it.
Lucy knows that Paul thinks she does not know about it.

Or even worse, if you really want a headache:

Lucy is still having that video.
She knows about it.
Paul knows about it.
She thinks Paul does not know she knows about it.
Paul knows she thinks he does not know she knows about it!

Had enough?

The child in the classroom

Such awareness of others' thinking is not just important in odd situations and problems like these, however. In actual classroom learning, teachers want children to appreciate why others think the way they do during a discussion, or when they encourage empathy with a character in a story. Similarly, in history and geography it does not really matter whether they study the Incas as opposed to the Aztecs, for example, because what teachers really want is for children to come to appreciate the values of people far removed from themselves in space or time, and thus eventually to become more aware of their own culture.

   Social understandings are not restricted to knowledge, of course. In order to survive in school, children also have to learn many rules, but teachers may not always make our expectations clear, so that children also have to cope with the social requirements of 'the hidden curriculum'. The inappropriate responses of young children who are just learning these rules can thus be very revealing. For instance, in Cameo 2, the children sat up ridiculously straight, with arms folded very high, almost rising out of their seats in an attempt to show the teacher how incredibly good they were being! They have come to associate a certain posture with 'being good' in order to win the teacher's approval. (In view of what was said in Chapter 3, it is also significant that they fasten on to the most concrete and enactive aspects of being good.) Similarly, they may come to ask a question and will raise their hand even though they are standing right next to the teacher. They have learned that they *have* to put their hand up to talk to a teacher, but have not yet learned when this social rule is inappropriate.

In some cases, children may even misbehave because they do not really understand the unwritten social rules of the classroom, or because the implicit classroom rules differ from the ones they are used to at home. Lund (1996) thus proposes that teachers should consider behaviour not as good or bad, but as appropriate or inappropriate in a particular social context. One of the main themes of Chapter 2 concerned making thinking more explicit, and many approaches to class management similarly suggest that teachers begin by discussing these rules and making them explicit to the extent of putting them up on the wall.

Nor is it enough for children to learn a single set of social rules, since they obviously change according to the situation. Acceptable behaviour in the playground may clearly be unacceptable in the classroom, and experts in children's behaviour emphasize the need to look at the specific *contexts* in which behaviour occurs. A common framework is to consider:

A the Antecedents of the behaviour.
B the exact nature of the Behaviour itself.
C the Consequences of the behaviour.

(See, for example, Ayers *et al.* 1995)

Many teachers feel that they really get to know their children during the very different social circumstances of a school trip, especially a residential one where relationships can be more relaxed (if 'relaxed' is an appropriate word to use about a residential trip!). Less obviously, there are different expectations about behaviour according to the subject area or activity, so that children may be expected to listen to instructions in silence one minute and yet reveal their innermost feelings publicly the next. In a class discussion, for instance, children need to learn skills such as:

- How to express their feelings.
- Listening to others and taking turns.
- Giving feedback and encouragement.
- Making use of feedback from others.
- Being aware of their own and others' non-verbal communication.

Teachers may also expect children to make a subtle distinction between learning, where the rule is 'do as you think' and behaviour, where the rule is 'do as I say' (Galton 1995). Such complex interpersonal skills can be seen in conjunction with the intrapersonal awareness of one's own feelings already discussed in the context of Gardner's (1983) theory of multiple intelligences. Both are essential to classroom learning, even though they appear to have low status in the National Curriculum (Hall 1994).

Children's groups

Classes themselves, or other groups of children in school, are also an important part of the social context of learning, and the effects of the peer group increase as children grow older and become more aware of their individual and group identities. One way of trying to chart the complex social relationships between children in a class is to use a sociogram. The technique consists simply of asking each child confidentially to name the child in the group whom they like best, or would most like to work with, then putting all the names on a diagram with lines to indicate each choice. It can be quite revealing, but care is needed. In particular:

- Remember that an exercise like this can be potentially threatening to some children, and needs careful handling. Even when I demonstrate sociograms with groups of teachers, I never use their names, but get them to nominate famous people instead, as shown in Figure 5.1 (see page 100).

- The children's choices must therefore be totally confidential. They will ask, of course, and may bargain with each other – 'I'll put you if you put me'. This may be impossible to prevent, and it can actually be quite revealing.
- It is better to have a particular question like 'Who is your best friend in the class?' or 'Who would you like to sit next to when we do project work?'
- It is simpler to ask just for the first choice. Getting a second choice can be interesting, but it makes for a very complicated diagram.
- If choices outside the class are allowed, it may also be revealing, as when a child chooses someone considerably younger, but it will not be helpful if the choice is someone the teacher does not know, or even someone who goes to a different school!
- Normally, it is not a good idea to ask who their least favourite person is, especially if the teacher is trying to promote a supportive and cohesive group feeling, as will be discussed later.

Suppose for example your slightly unusual class consisted of Lady Godiva, Hitler, Donald Duck, Queen Victoria, Marilyn Monroe, Shakespeare and Adam and Eve, and they made the following choices:

Hitler chose Lady Godiva

Lady Godiva, Queen Victoria and Shakespeare all chose Donald Duck

Donald Duck chose Queen Victoria

Adam and Eve chose each other

Marilyn Monroe chose Adam

Once the choices are made, the diagram can be produced (see Figure 5.1). Most people find that their first attempt is rather messy, with some very long lines, and may need to be re-drawn. Some points to look out for on the diagram are:

- *Stars* (e.g. Donald Duck): these are children who are chosen by more than one other child. Are some of them obvious leaders of groups, and if so, is there anything that binds the group together? Who have the stars chosen? For instance, is there an obvious second in command?

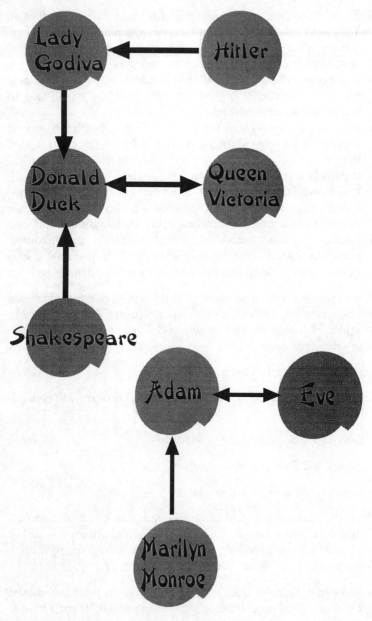

Figure 5.1 Friendship choices among a rather unusual group of people!

- *Isolates* (e.g. Hitler): these are children who are not chosen by anybody. Are they obvious loners, or are there any surprises? Who did the isolates choose – popular children or not?
- *Mutual pairs* (e.g. Adam and Eve): these are children who both choose each other. Are they at the centre of a group, or would they have been isolates if they had not chosen each other?
- *Subgroups* (e.g. Adam, Eve and Marilyn Monroe): does your class fall into two or more distinct subgroups with no links between them? In practice, for example, boys and girls will often form separate groups. If one single choice links what would otherwise have been separate groups, look at the child who makes the link and consider their position in the class.

The technique is particularly useful for getting to know more about a new class, though if the children are familiar, it is also interesting to see if the results are predictable. It may also help you to understand some of their behaviour. For example, I once realized that a boy who had recently started behaving badly was an isolate trying to gain acceptance into a group of rather disaffected boys. Such information can help with the planning of group work, for instance, or wise teachers will use it to ensure that they get the stars on their side!

Finally, do remember that children's friendship choices are notoriously fickle, and that if the exercise is repeated a week later, there could be several changes, especially with young children (this in itself would be interesting of course). For a more detailed discussion, see Smith (1993).

Learning about the wider social context

In order to learn successfully in school, children have to develop an awareness of what some psychologists call 'scenarios' or 'scripts'. McShane (1991) notes that these include not only different school settings, but also the sequence of expected behaviour during a visit to a restaurant, for instance. I am slightly amused if my son innocently orders his sweet at the same time as his main course, and he would feel utterly publicly humiliated at McDonald's if I went straight to a table and asked for a waiter to bring some cutlery! Hudson (1993) discusses how such 'script knowledge' develops and supports the emergence of more complex cognitive processes which eventually become disembedded from specific situations, in line with what was said in Chapter 2 about the development from concrete to abstract thought. (Remember the paper-folding?) So here again, social awareness is inextricably bound up with individual cognitive development.

In turn, the particular contexts of scripts are themselves part of a wider social context which reflects the values of the culture as a whole. For instance, in the West, each person at the restaurant orders their own individual meal, whereas in China, all dishes are placed in the centre and shared, reflecting 'individualist' and 'collectivist' values respectively. Such differences are also apparent in more subtle forms, such as the socially acceptable ways of presenting ourselves, or even the distance we stand apart from others when talking. Children have to learn not only about acceptable behaviour, but also about the underlying values that the behaviour represents, such as being considerate or not showing off (see Myers 1995: Ch. 19 for further discussion).

Parents, home and real-life learning

Of course, much of this learning has taken place well before children arrive at school. Most teachers now recognize that parents are the child's first teachers, and children's behaviour in school is often clearly modelled on what they have seen at home, so that meeting parents for the first time can certainly give insights into why their children act the way they do. The detailed scenarios of home and school are very different: if we take eating as an example again, the child's first school dinner is a completely different experience from previous mealtimes at home. But if underlying expectations about behaviour at home match expectations of school behaviour (for example asking for something to be passed to you, or waiting your turn), the child is bound to get off to a better start than if the two sets of expectations are different.

Indeed, some have argued that the parent at home provides better learning environment than the teacher at school. Wood (1991) describes school learning as 'contrived' and dependent on the teacher, in contrast to home learning, which he sees as 'spontaneous' and dependent on the child's needs. Similarly, Cockburn (1995) says that what goes on in many classrooms is geared to being favourably assessed and to pleasing the teacher, so that children may seem to be working hard while actually learning

Children's behaviour in school is often clearly modelled on what they have seen at home

little. The comparison between teachers and parents is not an entirely fair one, however, since most parents would probably prefer not to have another 29 children as well as their own, or to have to produce detailed objectives and plans before playing with their child. The difference is due not to the inadequacy or insensitivity of teachers as opposed to parents, but to the constraints which the culture places on its formal institutionalized education.

Cultural pressures do also act on parents when they teach their own children, but in less explicit ways. Mercer (1995) discusses how different societies have different expectations of how children should learn at home. For instance, parents in Zimbabwe use 'education by recitation', playing games which involve reciting lists of important names together with their children. Elsewhere, strong traditions of learning from story-telling encourage a more receptive and less questioning attitude in children, recognizing and accepting the authority of the adult. In other cultures, such attitudes might conflict with a desire to encourage children to be more questioning and to function independently of the teacher (David and Palincsar 1994).

Ultimately, however, schools are not created solely as social institutions in their own right, but to prepare children for life outside school, both as children now and as adults later. This can prove difficult if we accept the point made in Chapter 3 that much of children's learning is 'situated' or tied to the particular contexts in which it occurs, so that an important function of school learning is to help children to go beyond the immediate classroom context and to learn in ways that are disembedded or decontextualized, so that what they learn will generalize and transfer to other situations.

It does seem common sense that children should learn at school things that will be directly useful to them outside, yet this may not always happen. For example, consider the sort of shop usually set up in classrooms for young children, where one child acts as the shopkeeper and the other as the customer. The customer asks for various things, which the shopkeeper gets for them, followed by payment and perhaps the giving of change. This is a rich social situation with plenty of potential for language and number development, but it is nothing like most children's experience of real shopping with their parents. The two scenarios are completely different.

Similarly, older children may be expected to calculate accurately the total area of the walls of a room because this is seen as a useful thing to be able to do. We feel that an adult *ought* to be able to do such calculations, and if pushed to say exactly why it is useful, most teachers would answer in terms of decorating or something similar. Yet in real life an adult who needs to buy wallpaper does not do this at all. They will probably measure the height of the room, then round it up to the nearest easy number. There is no need to measure around the walls because it is much quicker to count the number of existing 'drops' of wallpaper. They then work out a very rough estimate of the number of rolls they will need, probably adding an extra roll to allow for waste, and maybe pessimistically another roll on top of that to allow for mistakes. At no time is there any accurate calculating required.

However, even when activities in and out of school directly match each other, the classroom context still makes a difference. This was particularly vividly illustrated by some research by Carraher *et al.* (1990) in Brazil. The researchers observed young street vendors selling drinks, sweets and cigarettes, rapidly calculating totals and effortlessly giving correct change. Yet when these same children were presented with exactly the same calculations later as pencil and paper problems to be solved in school, they were unable to do them! Desforges (1995) thus argues that teachers need to teach 'application strategies' to bridge the gaps between the skills taught in school and the skills required in real life.

This first section has looked at some aspects of the various social contexts in which children learn. Clearly, teachers too operate in such contexts, and the next section turns to consider the different ways in which social factors affect teaching.

The teacher

Teacher roles and role conflict

All primary teachers recognize the variety of roles they take on in an average day. They include accountant, nurse, detective, judge, counsellor, social worker, actor, walking dictionary and many others, and that's just during registration! Such complex interpersonal roles represent one of the reasons why it is so difficult to describe a successful teacher in terms of behavioural competencies. To be fair, teaching is not the only job which demands such a range of roles. I once gave a presentation to a group of medical officers about training their staff and, foolishly looking for sympathy, mentioned the number of roles that a teacher takes on, only to be told that for them, teaching was just one of many roles and that they also had to be accountants, judges, social workers, counsellors, walking medical dictionaries and so on!

Teachers normally slip automatically from one role to another, but they may occasionally become only too aware of what they are doing when one role conflicts with another – when the desire to help a child through a difficult emotional period clashes with the need for control, or when tight budgets prevent them from giving every child the materials they would like.

Teacher status

Even teachers who see themselves as models of democracy have responsibilities in the classroom which mean that their status must be different from that of the children. This can be difficult at first: one common problem faced by student teachers is that, because they like children, they very much want children to like them. Moreover, when they first go into classrooms, they often do so as helpers rather than teachers, and can be seen by the children as 'big friends', leading to all sorts of problems when they eventually try to take on the role of teacher, with resentment on both sides.

As teachers we unconsciously reinforce our social status in a number of ways, including ones enshrined in the unwritten rules discussed above. The teacher can usually do many things that the children normally cannot, such as:

- go anywhere in the room at any time;
- write on the board;
- sit on a chair rather than the floor;
- interrupt (oh yes you do!);
- allocate praise and criticism;
- use everybody's first name;
- write on other people's work;
- use certain resources or equipment;
- generally decide who does what.

Status can be reinforced in numerous small ways, too. For instance, take something apparently very straightforward, such as helping an individual child with their work. One way is for the teacher to summon the child to the teacher's table and remain seated while the child stands – a typical pattern for indicating high and low status. If you doubt this, think how you would behave if an Ofsted inspector came up to your table while you were sitting there. You would probably give up your 'superior' position and stand up to acknowledge their status, then maybe both sit down together.

The teacher's power can also be reinforced in more subtle ways. For instance, another common technique is for the teacher to select an individual or group and go over to help them. It may seem that the status positions are now reversed, with the child sitting and the teacher standing, but here again it is the teacher, not the child, who has set up the interaction (though the child may have requested it by raising their hand). The hidden message is that the teacher can go anywhere in the room at any time, while the child has to wait for the teacher. Moreover, the teacher decides exactly where to stand, and will often take up a position behind the child so that their work is easy to see. While this seems reasonable and allows the teacher to watch the rest of the class, it also puts them in a powerful position psychologically because the teacher can see the child, but not vice versa. Again, if you think this is an exaggeration, think how you would react if a child came to see you at your table and stood behind you in this way.

Experienced teachers will keep glancing away from the child while they are speaking to them, to monitor the rest of the class, though some beginner teachers find it hard to change their normal social behaviour in this way. It would certainly be unacceptable for a child to do this, and in the army they would probably put you on a charge for 'dumb insolence'!

Teacher talk

The roles and status of the teacher are therefore made apparent in many ways in the classroom, and this is particularly true with teacher talk. In an attempt to involve children as actively as possible, most British primary teachers do not just lecture the whole class from the front, but also make use of 'class discussions'. However, analysis of such sessions shows that they are not really discussions at all, as some of us may have found to our cost when we have inadvertently talked to friends or family in the same way in which we have been talking to children!

A typical exchange in a classroom 'discussion' tends to fall into three parts:

- *Initiation* by the teacher, often in the form of a question inviting children to respond.
- *Response* from a child selected by the teacher, often on the basis of a raised hand.
- *Follow-up* by the teacher, often repeating, evaluating or enlarging upon what the child has said.

Cameo 1 illustrated this pattern clearly, and it is significant that neither the teacher nor the children saw anything odd about it at the time. The exchange was also an example of the classic classroom game of 'guessing what's on the teacher's mind', and it confirmed the social role of the teacher as the person who knows all the answers but asks all the questions. This picture may seem familiar, though the immediate reaction of most teachers (including mine) is to deny that their own class discussions are ever as rigid or teacher-controlled as that! However, most become convinced after tape recording, or a little honest reflection, and the next reaction is usually to maintain that the pattern is unavoidable given the constraints of the classroom and the need to maintain at least some status and control. But is it?

Teaching and learning in conflict?

Teachers face a dilemma which reflects a major issue at the very heart of teaching and learning. On the one hand, most Western teachers recognize a view of children's learning which puts the individual first, with an emphasis on the active processing of information which is socially mediated through other people. On the other hand, being a teacher in the culturally-defined setting of the classroom means taking on certain roles and status which seem to inhibit real learning because the individual child is just one of a large group whose learning must be planned, organized, managed and monitored by the teacher.

The final section of this chapter explores some ideas for trying to resolve this apparent dilemma between the nature of learning and the demands of teaching, within the context of the classroom.

The context

Questions and wait-time

Let us begin by considering a change which is not too radical, which poses no threat to the status of the teacher, and which even preserves the classic teacher/pupil/teacher three part interchange. In several studies, Rowe (e.g. 1986) found that the time teachers wait at various points in the classic three-part exchange outlined above is very short indeed – often no more than a second or two. (You may find that rather surprising, in which case you might consider getting out the tape recorder again.) She then encouraged teachers to wait for even just a few extra seconds at each stage – before asking a question, after asking a question but before deciding who would respond, and after the child's response. This simple change produced some very positive results, including the following:

- Children spoke for longer and with more confidence.
- There were fewer occasions when there was no response.
- Children spoke spontaneously more often.
- Children responded to each other more, rather than just to the teacher.

Nor were all the benefits limited to the quality of what the children said: teachers found that they asked fewer questions but better and more varied ones, and that they found themselves answering their own questions less often!

The clear implication is that the children's thinking (and the teacher's) benefitted from having more time to reflect. This would certainly be in keeping with the evidence of cognitive psychologists. It is well established that many children rely heavily on visual images, and that such images may take several seconds to be formed, controlled and manipulated (Paivio 1986).

We will ask the questions!

Even with longer wait-times, the teacher is still the person who asks the questions and evaluates the answers, but there could be benefits from changing this classic pattern of social exchange even more radically. Tizard and Hughes (1984) note that pre-school children learn by asking adults lots of questions, but this pattern is quickly reversed once they come to school, while Wood (1988) argues that constant teacher questions can actually limit real learning and inhibit the development of higher-order thinking skills.

To be fair, the social situations of home and school are very different, and teacher questions are of course very useful, helping to maintain attention as well as to monitor children's learning, but they need not be restricted to the classic format already discussed. For instance:

- Instead of the teacher always setting the questions, children can set them for each other. They could be quiz questions on a project, or 'comprehension' questions on a particular text. Changing the format not only gives a purpose and audience to the activity but also means that the children will have to think carefully about the information they have, and will not be able simply to copy out a few lines that look vaguely relevant.

- Children can be challenged to think up different sorts of questions, such as ones where everybody would give the same answer, and ones where people could give different answers without being wrong. In doing so, they will be beginning to think about inferences or value judgements.
- Teachers can give children some questions *before* they get the information, to give more purpose to the activity or, better still, encourage them to think up their own first. What would they like to find out?
- Similarly, children can ask someone else questions to find out about something such as a book, using the '20 questions' format, where only the answers 'yes' and 'no' are allowed.

Moving away from questions

Questions can sometimes be replaced with something else, especially where the children may feel that they really can contribute, for example by talking about their own experiences. For instance, instead of leading a 'discussion' about bonfire night through a series of questions, the teacher could simply suggest that the group talks about it. After a time, if nothing is forthcoming, try a statement rather than a question, like 'When I was little I used to like the bonfire but I always felt a bit sorry for the guy', then wait again. It will probably take some time for older children to get used to such a change, though most young children are constantly bursting to tell us about everything – the more irrelevant it is, the keener they seem to be to tell us about it! With older children, on the other hand, it may be easier for the teacher to discuss openly what they are trying to do.

Think too what it is like to be 'on the receiving end' as a learner in similar situations. For instance, I have noticed that when I am running a workshop and a group of teachers are having a lively discussion, if I go to join them, my supposedly encouraging, open-ended question 'How's it going then?' is like the kiss of death to the entire discussion! Then when somebody does say something, they almost invariably address it to me rather than the rest of the group. The pressures on children to act in similar ways are probably much stronger, given the differences in roles and the much more obvious distinctions in status already mentioned.

So how can we begin to change this sort of response? One way is simply for the teacher not to join small group discussions at all, as Sotto (1994) recommends. I have done this with groups of teachers, and found it embarrassingly difficult at first! I hovered around pathetically, hoping that some group would ask me to join them, but they rarely did, and their discussions seemed none the worse for it. However, teachers may well feel that this is not a realistic option, given the different skills and needs of children as opposed to adult learners, plus other aspects of the role as teacher such as the need to assess children's learning.

So if you do sit in on a group, try to use your awareness of non-verbal skills, such as eye contact. If a child says something which is not a direct answer to a question of yours, they will still probably look at you to gauge your response, maintaining the classic teacher/pupil/teacher interchange. Do not comment on their contribution and try deliberately not returning their eye contact. Instead, grunt and nod in a vaguely encouraging way (as you might with another adult) and gaze into the middle distance to show you are considering carefully what they say, looking thoughtful and approving but acting as if you are just another member of the group. This may sound a trivial change, but both you and they may find it surprisingly disconcerting at first because it breaks another of those implicit social rules.

Group work

Many people have written about collaborative group work, ranging from those who see it as the only vehicle for real learning to those who regard it as responsible for the collapse of Western civilization as we know it. Whatever your views, true collaborative work means more than children just sitting round tables rather than in rows, and the skills involved need to be built up over time (Galton 1995; Bennett 1995).

Johnson and Johnson (1994) consider that the essence of collaborative learning is that there should be some sort of controversy or challenge, with alternative viewpoints actively promoted within a cooperative framework, while Mercer (1995) proposes three kinds of talk in groups:

- *Disputational* where individuals simply present their own views and refuse to listen to the ideas of others, so that no learning takes place (the House of Commons would be a particularly fine example).

- *Cumulative* where everybody agrees, but discussion is uncritical, so that again nothing is learned (as at Party Conferences).
- *Exploratory* which combines both criticism and agreement to foster real thinking and learning (significantly, no political parallel springs to mind).

Such views reveal interesting links with what was said about the nature of individual learning in Chapters 1–3, and in many ways dialogue can be seen as making thought public and explicit, in line with the views of Vygotsky. Similarly, in the terms of Piaget mentioned in Chapter 3, Mercer's 'exploratory' talk encourages learning because it combines assimilation and accommodation, respectively supporting and challenging existing ideas.

Given these ideas about collaborative group work, what sorts of strategies can teachers try within the normal classroom context? One common technique is 'circle time', where teacher and children all sit in a large circle, and where the change in seating acts as a clear signal that different sorts of social rules now apply. Possible activities include:

- Encouraging everybody both to speak and to listen by using an object to pass round, like the conch in Golding's *Lord of the Flies*. Only the person holding the object can speak, and children may of course literally 'pass' and not say anything if they prefer.
- Remembering and sharing a good time.
- Making positive comments about another member of the group.
- Completing a sentence such as 'I feel happy/angry/silly/upset when . . .'

Significantly, such group activities are particularly effective in improving self-esteem, but they need not take place *only* in circle time. Other small group activities which could form part of a curriculum project and which encourage self-esteem as well as genuine collaborative learning include:

- *Tribes*: these are groups of half a dozen children who deliberately support each other through explicit rules about confidentiality, listening, the right to silence and so on (Fisher 1995). Such groups will be fostered in cultures where group membership is seen as important. Lewis (1995) reports on the widespread use of small *han* groups in Japan where small subgroups of 4–8 children of deliberately mixed ability work and do social activities together, such as sharing out the food at lunch time, but they could just as easily be developed from the way many British classrooms are organized around differ ent tables of children.

- *Experts*: the group is given something to plan (such as going on an overnight hike) and each member is assigned an expert role (such as expert cook, route planner or camper). Experts have to be consulted when relevant, and nobody is allowed to question their decisions.
- *Jigsaws*: the group again plan or create something jointly, but each member has some information which nobody else has, forcing them to collaborate.
- *Jigsaw relays*: the group work on a problem in stages. When they have solved each stage, members take it in turn to go to the teacher to get the next bit of the problem, and have to present it to the rest.
- *Tournaments*: in other cultures where competition is encouraged, such groups may also be used to introduce a competitive element as well as a cooperative one. Thus in the USA, Slavin (1983) developed a number of techniques for working in such groups, including 'tournaments' where matched individuals from different teams compete with each other.

Promoting class community

Ideas like these can help to improve both individual self-esteem and collaboration in groups, but it is also valuable to try to promote a feeling of cohesion and identity within the whole class or teaching group. Bruner (1996) discusses how cultures produce collective '*œuvres*' or 'works' in the form of arts or sciences, laws or versions of history. There are many ways of promoting group identity, and a class can develop a similar feeling of cohesion through producing class assembly, or by taking pride in having the tidiest classroom, or by deliberately cultivating private jokes or sayings. This can also involve individual self-esteem by promoting Donna as the *class* computer expert or Sanjit as *our* best joke-teller, encouraging individuals to feel valued as part of the group.

There are many ways of promoting group identity!

The notion of a 'community of enquiry' is one of the best-known approaches to setting up a class atmosphere in which genuine discussion can occur (Lipman *et al.* 1980; see also Fisher 1995). Most children seem able to benefit from and in time can take an active part in 'philosophical' discussions that promote real learning, though care is perhaps needed in deciding exactly what factors bring about the changes (Lake 1996).

One factor does seem to be the willingness to take on a different sort of role, as a mediator rather than a leader, in line with the earlier discussion about the roles and status of the teacher generally. A similar approach is advocated by Brown and Palincsar (1989) in what they call 'reciprocal teaching', where the teacher initially acts a model, after which pupils take it in turn to lead the group through four stages of discussion:

- Question posed by the leader.
- Clarification and discussion by the group.
- Summary from the leader.
- Group decision on future content.

For further discussion and evaluation of reciprocal teaching, see McGilly (1994).

Moving on

This chapter has shown how the social contexts of learning are not simply background features which we can choose to ignore. Social factors are often not made explicit, but they have major effects on both teaching and learning, both in and out of school, and at all levels ranging from the macro context of a culture's values to the micro context of an individual's behaviour in the classroom. Social factors also interact with children's and teachers' attitudes and with the cognitive aspects of learning which were the focus of earlier chapters. The final chapter will look at the nature of some of these interactions to consider what goes into making teaching and learning successful.

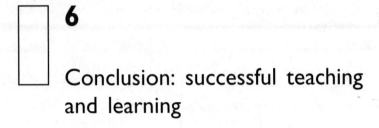

6

Conclusion: successful teaching and learning

The story so far

We have seen so far that classroom success cannot be adequately described or promoted by studying observable behaviour alone, and that behavioural competences can thus be of only limited value. We must also try to understand what might be going on inside teachers' and children's heads, while recognizing that we can only make inferences from what we can observe. Nor is it enough to consider only the cognitive processes of teachers and learners, since we must also take into account their attitudes and feelings, and the social contexts in which they operate.

This concluding chapter will combine these factors to outline an overall picture of what seems to be involved in successful teaching and learning, based on two overlapping themes which run through the book. Each theme can be represented by a continuum:

Safety and security > Challenge and risk
Public knowledge > Private understanding

'Comfortable challenge'

One theme which has emerged in several different ways has been the notion that successful learning takes place when the child is encouraged to take risks and be open to new problems in a secure environment, where lack of immediate success does not pose a personal threat. This dynamic interaction between risk and security is neatly summed up in the phrase 'comfortable challenge', and it has appeared as a theme in several previous chapters.

In Chapter 2 I suggested that the need to overcome our limitations as information processors and actively to seek out intellectual challenge is at the heart of learning. As my boyhood hero Sherlock Holmes put it in *The Sign of Four*:

> 'My mind,' he said, 'rebels at stagnation. Give me problems, give me work, give me the most abstruse cryptogram, or the most intricate analysis, and I am in my own proper atmosphere . . . But I abhor the dull routine of existence. I crave for mental exaltation.'
>
> (Conan Doyle 1981: 89)

On the other hand, the goal of all this 'mental exaltation' is not to make life difficult, but to reduce the problem to something we can understand, and this central search after meaning represents the other half of the dynamic relationship between comfort and challenge.

Chapter 3 explored how this same interaction is vital in children's cognitive development, and Piaget's terms 'assimilation' and 'accommodation' can be seen very much in this way. Assimilation represents the security of established concepts which allow us to use our past experience to deal with the world, while accommodation represents the need to modify those concepts in the light of the new experiences which successful learners actively seek out.

In Chapter 4, we saw how successful learning requires not only cognitive skills but also appropriate attitudes towards the task and towards ourselves as learners. Children who exhibit the range of attitudes known as mastery orientation are certainly willing to risk being wrong and actually relish the effort needed to solve a new problem, while the solution itself represents a new level of 'safety' in which the new knowledge or skill is added to their repertoire. Fox (1995) notes a similar balance in terms of attitudes – new material must be sufficiently challenging to avoid boredom, but not so challenging that it leads to a loss of confidence and an unwillingness to engage.

Teachers trying to maintain this balance will therefore need to consider far more than the sorts of observable products that can be described in behavioural competences. In fact, they will constantly be trying to provide what Bruner calls 'scaffolding' – temporary support which enables the child to take on an active role in the development of their own understanding (Bruner and Haste 1987). Thus the successful teacher does not simply *present* information, even a bit at a time as in a behavioural programme; instead, they *intervene* in the child's learning. Like many other ideas in education, this sounds splendid, but what exactly might it mean in practice?

Adey and Shayer (1994) strongly promote the notion of teacher intervention, and propose that it has six essential features:

- Density and duration – in other words, there needs to be lots of it!
- Concrete preparation, so that children recognize the importance to them of what is to be learned.
- Cognitive conflict, so that there is motivation to change their thinking.
- Construction zone, involving teacher mediation (see below).
- Metacognition, so that they become aware of their own thinking and able to monitor it.
- Bridging, to enable them to transfer and generalize what they have learned to other contexts.

A key concept here is the 'construction zone' in which teacher and child work together to produce joint understandings of what is being learned. This sounds very laudable, but it is again fair to ask what it might mean in practice. According to what seems appropriate to children's needs at the time, the teacher might try various techniques, all of which have arisen in previous chapters:

- Listen to the children to find out about their current understanding, or use other ways of making it explicit, such as mind maps.
- Ask questions to check on this understanding and to point out mismatches.
- Direct the children's attention to particular aspects of the materials or activity – the 'significant features', such as the word at the top of each page in the dictionary.
- Remind children about relevant events or findings from the past.
- Encourage children to make hypotheses or predictions.
- Amplify what the children say and involve them in dialogue.

- Model various courses of action, using expert protocols and similar devices.
- Suggest strategies to help the children to learn and to build mental models.
- Draw attention to the results of the children's activity, as feedback.
- Encourage the children to suggest different possible ways to proceed.
- Allow the children space and time to try things out without any teacher intervention!

Overall, the successful teacher therefore offers a challenge to the child's thinking in a way that does not pose a threat to their security. In the long run, the aim is to encourage children spontaneously to take on such roles for themselves, internalizing the questioning, hypothesizing and so on to provide the 'scaffolding' for themselves.

Another way of looking at this complex learning relationship is through Vygotsky's much-quoted term the 'zone of proximal development' (ZPD – see Newman *et al.* 1989 for a particularly detailed discussion). Here, the role of the adult is to help the child eventually achieve for themselves what they can currently achieve only with support. Again, it is fair to ask what this might mean in practice. Tharp and Gallimore (1991) propose four stages of 'assisted performance' where the teacher offers support or scaffolding to help the child to move on through the ZPD.

Stage one

To begin with, the child is assisted by a teacher or some other person who is more capable than the child. Significantly, the teacher's role here is not to simplify the task and to break it down into small, easily achievable steps in order to 'shape' the child's performance, as it would be in a behavioural programme. Instead, the aim is to simplify the child's role in the task. The adult therefore begins by offering the minimum help or cues they think necessary, increasing the support as appropriate, so that their input depends not on the predetermined steps of the programme but on the current performance of the child. This first stage would therefore involve the sorts of teacher interventions outlined above.

Stage two

So far, much of what has gone on has been observable, though the teacher is of course constantly making inferences about the child's thinking (and the child is probably making inferences about what the teacher is getting at!) The next stages involve this behaviour becoming internalized and no longer observable, so to understand better what happens next, try doing the subtraction problem below in your head:

5038 −
3974

You probably had no difficulty with this, but were you aware of saying anything to yourself in your head for at least part of it? Given such a problem, rather to my embarrassment, I sometimes find myself chanting something like, 'seven from three you can't, so borrow one, seven off the ten leaves three, three and three are six'. I am even more likely to go through some similar rigmarole when I come to a really tricky bit like trying to 'borrow' from the hundreds column when it consists of a zero. Real mathematicians would be appalled, but I suspect that 'Maggie' Mercer (my teacher at King Street Primary at the beginning of Chapter 1) and the other teachers there would be proud of me!

This example illustrates the second stage neatly. The child is encouraged to support their own performance by means of self-instruction to replace the adult's instructions or commentary. In a way, the child is thus beginning to take responsibility for the metacognitive aspects of the task. Here, according to Vygotsky, as we saw in Chapter 3, the verbal support may still be needed, but it will now be sub-vocal, or take the form of speech 'inside the head'. On the other hand, the fact that it is necessary at all means that it is taking up a lot of thinking capacity and, as we saw in Chapter 2, this capacity is in fact very limited, so this is by no means the final stage.

Stage three

I don't always find myself chanting childish self-instructions learned decades ago in order to solve simple problems in my head. In the example above, I find I can immediately subtract the

4 from the 8 so quickly that I'm not aware of how I did it. Perhaps more interestingly, on other occasions, such as when playing darts, I realize I am also doing more complicated subtractions, such as 51−26, almost as automatically (though admittedly, I'm so awful at darts that I rarely have to subtract more than about 10 at a time!) On such occasions, my problem-solving has reached the third stage, where performance becomes so fluent and automatic that we are not normally aware of it at all. As we saw earlier, much of an expert's performance has reached this level, speeding up and using larger chunks of information to leave more thinking capacity available, but at the same time putting the performance beyond the reach of a learner.

Stage four

At this point, it may be necessary for the teacher to intervene again to take the child back to the ZPD with a new harder problem, encouraging them to talk it through and ask for help if necessary. For instance, a child who has learned to solve problems like:

58 −
39

Would probably need some support to solve:

614 −
287

And would almost certainly need help with problems like the first one above, involving zero. The adult's support is still vital, though it would of course be even better if the child could stop and reflect on their own performance, as we saw can happen in representational redescription, in Chapter 3.

Such steps reflect what most teachers would accept as good practice, but in the classroom it would seem impossible to give such sensitive individual support. However, the facilitator need not always be a teacher, of course, or even an adult, and many programmes actively encourage parents to become involved, or make use of peer partners. 'Paired reading' (Topping 1985), for example, uses several of these ideas. To begin with, the person in the tutor's role reads slowly but expressively, following the text with their finger as an extra visual signal to the learner. The same text may be read several times, and the learner encouraged to signal when they feel confident enough to take over the reading, signalling again when they need the tutor's help, so that the level of intervention is decided by the learner, not the teacher.

It will also be possible to make use of some of the ideas underlying these stages even when teaching a larger group, and some of those who advocate that we should at least consider more whole-class teaching deny that this means a total return to mass lectures delivered from the front, but should include lots of active participation from the children (Reynolds 1996). In order for this to work, however, it might be necessary to reconsider our ideas about differentiation and to try to reduce it rather than in effect increase it by catering for individual needs so much.

From what has been said so far about safety and risk, it will be apparent that we should avoid setting up another fruitless dichotomy, like several others mentioned previously, in which one side is seen as desirable and the other not. Willingness to take on the 'challenge' is not necessarily always a 'Good Thing'. It would be fruitless constantly to change our ideas in the face of insufficient evidence, or always to take on the challenge of learning something new regardless of the effort required.

Conversely, there is a danger that safety will be equated with a reluctance to tackle anything new, and it is true that safety must not be equated with rigidity or certainty that you are right. This danger is particularly apparent in a subject like science, where it seems to us that our current knowledge has replaced all the foolish ideas of our predecessors, and that we have now arrived at the Truth. It is a danger that was expressed powerfully and movingly by the scientist Jacob Bronowski as he knelt in the mud of Auschwitz concentration camp, where so many of his family died:

> We are always at the brink of the known, we always feel forward for what is to be hoped. Every judgement in science stands on the edge of error, and is personal. Science is a tribute to what we can know although we are fallible. In the end the words were said by Oliver Cromwell: 'I beseech you, in the bowels of Christ, think it possible you may be mistaken.'
>
> (Bronowski 1973: 374)

Public knowledge and private understanding

The notion of comfortable challenge is one which summarizes many of the ideas about successful teaching and learning which run through the first four chapters of this book, where the emphasis was particularly on individual learning. But we need also to consider the role of the teacher in its cultural context. The second dimension, with public knowledge at one end and private understanding at the other, does overlap with the notion of comfortable challenge, but the two are not the same. For 'private' thinking to be successful, it must involve elements of both safety and risk, and successful 'public' activity in the form of teaching equally requires both.

When we considered the social context of teaching and learning in Chapter 5, we saw how cultural pressures at the macro level can sometimes lead to a conservative emphasis in which the role of the school is simply to transmit established public knowledge to the next generation, in parallel with an emphasis on safety in individual thinking. This can raise difficult questions, however:

> Should schools aim to reproduce the culture, to 'assimilate' ... the young into the ways of being little Americans or little Japanese? Yet assimilation was the unexamined faith even as recently as the beginning of this century. Or would schools, given the revolutionary changes through which we are living, do better to dedicate themselves to the equally risky, perhaps equally quixotic ideal of preparing students to cope with the changing world in which they will be living?
>
> (Bruner 1996: ix)

We saw in Chapter 3 how these two contrasting views can be traced back to rationalist philosophy's emphasis on public knowledge on the one hand, and existentialist philosophy's belief in private self-awareness on the other. However, as with the other dichotomies we have explored, it is not the case that one view is simply correct and the other not, because successful teaching requires elements of both, as in Bonnett's (1994) notion of 'authentic-rational' thinking. Combining these two aspects thus means that the teacher acts as a mediator between the child's private understandings and the public demands of the curriculum.

In Britain, the advent of the National Curriculum was seen by many as a step away from child-centred learning towards the more public end of the continuum. Siraj-Blatchford and Siraj-Blatchford (1995: 1), for example, feel that 'the essential character of children's learning in the primary phase has been ignored by the introduction of a subject-based National Curriculum'. Cooper and McIntyre (1996) similarly consider the National Curriculum as prescriptive, not recognizing the child's prior knowledge and relegating the teacher to the role of deliverer. In this respect, the National Curriculum offers a distinctly uncomfortable challenge to teachers:

> The recent educational changes in England and Wales have been traumatic for many teachers and schools. They have raised basic questions of who they are, what they believe in, what aims they hold in life and how they are going to achieve them. Teachers' investment of their substantial selves into teaching has been challenged, as has their commitment to certain values, to their view of knowledge, to pupils, to teaching.
>
> (Woods 1995: 85)

While recognizing that the National Curriculum has brought some benefits, Woods goes on to describe how some schools are resisting through collaboration, or appropriating the National Curriculum to their own ends, and notes that teachers still have considerable room for manoeuvre when it comes to implementing it. Interestingly, the National Curriculum represents elements of both public security and private challenge. On the one hand it has meant an enforced radical shift towards publicly agreed content to be passed on to all children, but on the other hand it has presented most British teachers with a challenge to their previous notions of teaching based on their own individual professionalism. Many teachers are therefore refusing to accept the public requirements of the National Curriculum in a passive way, but are trying to modify it to be more compatible with their personal ideas of what successful teaching and learning are all about. In this respect, teachers too are trying to deal with potential conflict by transforming it into a comfortable challenge.

Putting it all together

Finally, putting the two dimensions together enables us to see how they relate to each other and acts as a summary of many of the main themes which run through this book. Taking each box shown in Table 6.1 briefly in turn, we can see how each combination represents a particular aspect of successful teaching and learning.

Public/safety

It is tempting to regard these aspects of teaching and learning as somehow less important than the others, and although it is true that an undue emphasis on cultural transmission would be damaging, institutionalized education clearly requires a strong element of stability. Chapter 1 showed how behavioural competences imply a restricted view of the nature of teaching and learning, but they can at least act as a framework for considering the content of what we think it is valuable for children to learn. Chapter 3 indicated how psychologists, having initially been more interested in cognitive processes, have increasingly recognized the importance of content and products as well, and are now finding out how knowledge interacts with the processes of learning. The National Curriculum has brought some advantages because it does go some way towards specifying what this publicly-agreed knowledge should be. At a different 'public' level, we have also seen how a supportive group or class identity can provide the sort of security which fosters successful learning.

Table 6.1

	Public	*Private*
Safety	National Curriculum, knowledge, cultural transmission, competences	Existing concepts, intuitive theories, assimilation
Challenge	Reflective practitioner, ZPD, dialogue, experiment	Mastery orientation, accommodation, risk-taking

Private/safety

At the level of the individual's 'private' learning, success depends on an interaction between stability and change, security and risk, or Piaget's assimilation and accommodation – a balance summed up in the phrase 'comfortable challenge'. Without concepts and intuitive theories, learners would not be able to make sense of the vast amounts of information presented by their senses, especially since this information tends to be partial, selective and fragmentary. Scenarios were offered as one example of the sorts of contextual understandings which successful learners acquire in order to deal with complex social situations. In terms of attitudes, the element of security implies a high level of self-esteem which gives children the self-confidence to be open to risk. Teachers will benefit from making their own and their children's existing ideas more explicit, and a willingness to accept challenge and risk does not mean that those ideas should always be taken on regardless of the effort needed and the likely consequences. At both the public and the private level, this conservative element may seem less exciting and dramatic than the aspects of learning which feature in the bottom two boxes, but it is just as essential.

Private/challenge

The aspects of learning represented in this box thus complement the conservative element by ensuring that the learner is open to challenge. If learning always involves some sort of change, then learners must recognize that there is a mismatch between their existing ideas and new information. Successful learners may question their ideas even when they appear to be perfectly adequate, with no external or 'public' mismatch, as in representational redescription. This in turn implies that learning is not restricted to cognitive skills, but involves a set of attitudes which prevent challenges from being seen as threatening. Moreover, successful learners, who exhibit such attitudes in mastery orientation, do not just accept cognitive challenge, but actively seek it out.

Public/challenge

Because almost all learning is socially mediated, the element of challenge needs also to find public expression. Previous chapters have suggested devices such as mind maps and expert protocols which can make both children's and teacher's thinking explicit, but dialogue and debate are even better because they not only make thinking public, but also encourage challenge. Johnson and Johnson (1994) thus claim that teachers should not try to avoid conflict, but should actively encourage it within a cooperative classroom context. Similarly, we have seen how the notion of a community of enquiry is not just about setting up a cosy 'community' atmosphere where nobody feels threatened. The 'enquiry' element of it means that ideas can be questioned and challenged as well as defended, and the atmosphere of a successful classroom is a public parallel of the comfortable challenge which enables individuals to learn.

Finalé

Previous chapters have used the device of separate sections focusing on the child and the teacher respectively for convenience, but ultimately, we clearly cannot consider teaching and learning as separate enterprises. Combining the elements of all four boxes in Table 6.1 means that the successful teacher generates comfortable challenges to mediate between their public knowledge of the curriculum and their private understanding of the child.

Successful teachers therefore cannot just be authorities, but need themselves to accept an element of challenge because this role of mediator implies that they must be willing to reflect on their practice. They need flexibility and a willingness to adapt their own ideas and skills to the child's thinking, rather than simply the ability to deliver the next page of the textbook. Both teacher and child are therefore like experimenters in many ways, engaged in collaborative research, producing hypotheses and trying them out, monitoring the results and modifying their ideas accordingly. A successful learning context is one where both the teacher and the child are secure enough to make their private thinking explicit and open to change, and successful teaching happens best when teachers too become more like successful learners.

References

Adey, P. and Shayer, M. (1994) *Really Raising Standards: Cognitive Intervention and Academic Achievement*. London: Routledge.

Ashman, A. and Conway, R. (1993) *Using Cognitive Methods in the Classroom*. London: Routledge.

Ayers, H., Clarke, D. and Murray, A. (1995) *Perspectives on Behaviour: a Practical Guide to Effective Interventions for Teachers*. London: David Fulton.

Bennett, M. (ed.) (1993) *The Child as Psychologist: an Introduction to the Development of Social Cognition*. New York: Harvester Wheatsheaf.

Bennett, N. (1995) Managing learning through group work, in C. Desforges (ed.) *An Introduction to Teaching: Psychological Perspectives*. Oxford: Blackwell.

Bethnal Green Centre Access Department (1987) *Cheating*. Self-published document.

Blagg, N., Ballinger, M. and Gardner, R. (1988) *Somerset Thinking Skills Course Handbook*. Oxford: Blackwell.

Bonnett, M. (1994) *Children's Thinking: Promoting Understanding in the Primary School*. London: Cassell.

Bransford, J. D., Vye, N. J., Adams, L. T. and Perfetto, G. A. (1989) Learning skills and the acquisition of knowledge, in A. Lesgold and R. Glaser (eds) *Foundations for a Psychology of Education*. Hillsdale NJ: Lawrence Erlbaum.

Bronowski, J. (1973) *The Ascent of Man*. London: BBC Books.

Brown, A. L. and Palincsar, A. S. (1989) Guided cooperative learning and individual knowledge acquisition, in L. Resnick (ed.) *Knowing and Learning: Issues for a Cognitive Psychology of Learning*. Hillsdale, NJ: Erlbaum.

Bruner, J. (1973) The growth of representational processes in childhood, in J. M. Anglin *Beyond the Information given: Studies in the Psychology of Knowing*. London: George Allen and Unwin.

Bruner, J. (1996) *The Culture of Education*. Cambridge, MA: Harvard University Press.

Bruner, J. and Haste, H. (eds) (1987) *Making Sense: the Child's Construction of the World*. London: Methuen.

Burden, B. and Florek, A. (1990) Instrumental enrichment, in V. Lee (ed.) *Children's Learning in School*. London: Hodder and Stoughton.

Butterworth, G. and Harris, M. (1994) *Principles of Developmental Psychology*. Hillsdale NJ: Lawrence Erlbaum.

Buzan, T. (1995) *Use Your Head*. London: BBC Books.

Carraher, T. N., Carraher, D. W. and Schliemann, A. D. (1990) Mathematics in the streets and in schools, in V. Lee (ed.) *Children's Learning in School*. London: Hodder and Stoughton.

Claxton, G. (1984) *Live and Learn: an introduction to the Psychology of Growth and Change in Everyday Life*. London: Harper and Row.

Claxton, G. (1996) Integrated learning theory and the learning teacher, in G. Claxton, T. Anderson, M. Osborn and M. Wallace (eds) *Liberating the Learner: Lessons for Professional Development in Education*. London: Routledge.

Claxton, G., Anderson, T., Osborn, M. and Wallace, M. (eds) (1996) *Liberating the Learner: Lessons for Professional Development in Education*. London: Routledge.

Cockburn, A. D. (1995) Learning in classrooms, in C. Desforges (ed.) *An Introduction to Teaching: Psychological Perspectives*. Oxford: Blackwell.

Conan Doyle, Sir A. (1981) *The Penguin Complete Sherlock Holmes*. Harmondsworth: Penguin.

Cooper, P. and McIntyre, D. (1996) *Effective Teaching and Learning: Teachers' and Students' Perspectives*. Buckingham: Open University Press.

Cullingford, C. (1991) *The Inner World of the School: Children's Ideas About Schools*. London: Cassell.

Das Gupta, P. and Richardson, K. (1995) Theories of cognitive development, in V. Lee and P. Das Gupta (eds) *Children's Cognitive and Language Development*. Oxford: Blackwell.

David, Y. M. and Palincsar, A. S. (1994) Cognitive strategy instruction: special education, in T. Husen and T.N. Postlethwaite (eds) *International Encyclopedia of Education*, 2nd edn. Oxford: Pergamon.

Department for Education (DfE) (1992) Circular 9/92 – *Initial teacher Training (Secondary Phase)*. London: HMSO.

Desforges, C. (ed.) (1995) *An Introduction to Teaching: Psychological Perspectives*. Oxford: Blackwell.

Donaldson, M. (1978) *Children's Minds*. Glasgow: Fontana.

Donaldson, M. (1992) *Human Minds: an Exploration*. London: Penguin.

Dougill, P. and Knott, R. (1988) *The Primary Language Book*. Milton Keynes: Open University Press.

Dweck, C. S. (1989) Motivation, in A. Lesgold and R. Glaser (eds) *Foundations for a Psychology of Education*. Hillsdale NJ: Lawrence Erlbaum.

Eisner, J. P. and Seligman, M. E. P. (1994) Self-related cognition, learned helplessness, learned optimism and human development, in T. Husen and T. N. Postlethwaite (eds) *International Encyclopedia of Education*, 2nd edn. Oxford: Pergamon.

Fisher, R. (1995) *Teaching Children to Learn*. Cheltenham: Stanley Thornes.

Fontana, D. (1995) *Psychology for Teachers*, 3rd edn. Basingstoke: Macmillan.

Foster, V. (1994a) Thinking allowed. *Special Children*, April: 12–14.

Foster, V. (1994b) Brill to the rescue. *Special Children*, May: 11–13.

Fox, R. (1995) Development and learning, in C. Desforges (ed.) *An Introduction to Teaching: Psychological Perspectives*. Oxford: Blackwell.

Galloway, D. and Edwards, A. (1991) *Primary School Teaching and Educational Psychology*. London: Longman.

Galton, M. (1995) *Crisis in the Primary Classroom*. London: David Fulton.

Galton, M. and Willcocks, J. (eds) (1983) *Moving from the Primary Classroom*. London: Routledge and Kegan Paul.

Gardner, H. (1983) *Frames of Mind: the Theory of Multiple Intelligences*. New York: Basic Books.

Gardner, H., Krechevsky, M., Sternberg, R. J. and Okagaki, L. (1994) Intelligence in context: enhancing students' practical intelligence for school, in K. McGilly (ed.) *Classroom Lessons: Integrating Cognitive Theory and Classroom Practice*. Cambridge, MA: MIT Press.

Gurney, P. (1988) *Self-esteem in Children with Special Educational Needs*. London: Routledge.

Halford, G. S. (1993) *Children's Understanding: the Development of Mental Models*. Hillsdale, NJ: Lawrence Erlbaum.

Hall, E. (1994) The social relational approach, in P. Kutnick and C. Rogers (eds) *Groups in Schools*. Cassell: London.

Hatano, G. (1994) Cognitive development and the acquisition of expertise, in T. Husen and T. N. Postlethwaite (eds) *International Encyclopedia of Education*, 2nd edn. Oxford: Pergamon.

Hawkins, C. (1995) Thinking straight. *Special Children*, February: 13–16.

Helmke, A. (1994) Self concept, development of, in T. Husen and T. N. Postlethwaite, *International Encyclopedia of Education* 2nd edn. Oxford: Pergamon.

Hodge, P. (1995) Carry one with a flash of the corsets, *Times Educational Supplement*, 22 September: 20.

Holt, J. (1991) *Learning all the Time*. Ticknall, Derbyshire: Education Now.

Howe, M. J. A. (1991) A fine idea but does it work? *British Psychological Society Education Section Review*, 15(2): 43–6.

Hudson, J. A. (1993) Script knowledge, in M. Bennett (ed.) *The Child as Psychologist: an Introduction to the Development of Social Cognition.* New York: Harvester Wheatsheaf.

Hunter-Grundin, E. (1985) *Teaching Thinking: an Evaluation of Edward de Bono's Classroom Materials.* London: Schools' Council/SCDC.

Hustler, D. and McIntyre, D. (eds) (1996) *Developing Competent Teachers: Approaches to Professional Competence in Teacher Education.* London: David Fulton.

Hyland, T. (1994) *Competence, Education and NVQs: Dissenting Perspectives.* London: Cassell.

Hyland, T. (1995) Behaviourism and the meaning of competence, in P. Hodkinson and M. Issitt (eds) *The Challenge of Competence.* London: Cassell.

Johnson, D. W. and Johnson, R. T. (1994) Collaborative learning and argumentation, in P. Kutnick and C. Rogers (eds) *Groups in Schools.* London: Cassell.

Johnson, G., Hill, B. and Tunstall, P. (1992) *Primary Records of Achievement: a Teachers' Guide to Reviewing, Recording and Reporting.* London: Hodder and Stoughton.

Jordan, R. and Powell, S. (1995) Skills without understanding: a critique of a competency-based model of teacher education in relation to special needs. *British Journal of Special Education* 22(3): 120–4.

Karmiloff-Smith, A. (1992) *Beyond Modularity.* Cambridge, MA: MIT Press.

Kessissoglou, S. and Farrell, P. (1996) Whatever happened to precision teaching? *British Journal of Special Education*, 22: 60–3.

Kitson, N. (1995) You don't know what you know 'til you know it! Competence-based teacher education, in J. Moyles (ed.) *Beginning Teaching: Beginning Learning in Primary Education.* Buckingham: Open University Press.

Kitson, N., and Merry, R. (1992) Is it a bird, is it a plane? Activities to encourage cognitive and language skills. *Language and Learning*, July: 5–7.

Kutnick, P. and Rogers, C. (1994) *Groups in Schools.* London: Cassell.

Kyriacou, C. (1995) Direct teaching, in C. Desforges (ed.) *An Introduction to Teaching: Psychological Perspectives.* Oxford: Blackwell.

Lake, M. (1996) Developing thinking skills, in P. Widlake (ed.) *The Good Practice Guide to Special Educational Needs.* Birmingham: Questions Publishing.

Lawrence, D. (1996) *Enhancing Self-esteem in the Classroom*, 2nd edn. London: Paul Chapman.

Lee, V. and Das Gupta, P. (1995) *Children's Cognitive and Language Development.* Oxford: Blackwell.

Leekham, S. (1993) Children's understanding of mind, in M. Bennett (ed.) *The Child as Psychologist: an Introduction to the Development of Social Cognition*. New York: Harvester Wheatsheaf.

Levin, J. R. (1993) Mnemonic strategies and classroom learning: a twenty year report card. *Elementary School Journal*, 94: 235–44.

Lewis, C. C. (1995) *Educating Hearts and Minds: Reflections on Japanese Pre-School and Elementary Education*. New York: Cambridge University Press.

Light, P. (1993) Developing psychologies, in M. Bennett (ed.) *The Child as Psychologist: an Introduction to the Development of Social Cognition*. New York: Harvester Wheatsheaf.

Light, P., Sheldon, S., and Woodhead, M. (eds) (1991) *Child Development in Social Context 2: Learning to Think*. London: Routledge.

Lipman, M., Sharp, A. and Oscanyan, F. (1980) *Philosophy in the Classroom*. Philadelphia, PA: Temple University Press.

Lund, R. (1996) *A Whole-School Behaviour Policy: a Practical Guide*. London: Kogan Page.

McGilly, K. (1994) *Classroom Lessons: Integrating Cognitive Theory and Classroom Practice*. Cambridge, MA: MIT Press.

McShane, J. (1991) *Cognitive Development: an Information-Processing Approach*. Oxford: Blackwell.

Mager, R. F. (1990) *Developing Attitude toward Learning or SMATS 'n' SMUTS*, 2nd edn. London: Kogan Page.

Mahoney, P. (1996) Competencies and the first year of teaching, in D. Hustler and D. McIntyre (eds) *Developing Competent Teachers: Approaches to Professional Competence in Teacher Education*. London: David Fulton.

Marsh, H. W. (1990) Causal ordering of academic self-concept and academic achievement: a multiwave, longitudinal panel analysis. *Journal of Educational Psychology*, 82: 646–56.

Meadows, S. (1993) *The Child as Thinker: the Development and Acquisition of Cognition in Childhood*. London: Routledge.

Mercer, N. (1995) *The Guided Construction of Knowledge: Talk Amongst Teachers and Learners*. Clevedon: Multilingual Matters.

Merrett, F. (1993) *Encouragement Works Best*. London: David Fulton.

Merry, R. (1992) Spelling strategies. *Language and Learning*, November: 14–16.

Merry, R. (1995) Take some notice of me! Primary children and their learning potential, In J. Moyles (ed.) *Beginning Teaching: Beginning Learning in Primary Education*. Buckingham: Open University Press.

Miller, G. (1956) The magical number seven, plus or minus two: some limits on our capacity for processing information. *Psychological Review*, 83: 81–7.

Morris, P. E. (1991) On M. Howe: learning to learn. *British Psychological Society Education Section Review*, 15: 49–50.

Myers, D. G. (1995) *Psychology*. New York: Worth.

Newman, D., Griffin, P. and Cole, M. (1989) *The Construction Zone: Working for Cognitive Change in School*. Cambridge: Cambridge University Press.

Norris, N. (1991) The trouble with competence. *Cambridge Journal of Education*, 21(3): 331–41.

O'Connor, J. and Seymour, J. (1993) *Neuro-Linguistic Programming: Psychological Skills for Understanding and Influencing People*. London: Aquarian.

Paivio, A. (1986) *Mental Representations: a Dual Coding Approach*. New York: Oxford University Press.

Perner, J. (1991) *Understanding the Representational Mind*. Cambridge, MA: MIT Press.

Pollard, A. and Filer, A. (1995) *The Social World of Children's Learning: Case Studies of Children from Four to Seven*. London: Cassell.

Pressley, M. and Van, P. (1994) Memory, teaching and testing for, in T. Husen and T. N. Postlethwaite (eds) *International Encyclopedia of Education*, 2nd edn. Oxford: Pergamon.

Resnick, L. B. (1987) *Education and Learning to Think*. Washington: National Academy Press.

Resnick, L.B. and Collins, A. (1994) Cognition and learning, in Husen, T. and Postlethwaite, T. N. (eds) *International Encyclopedia of Education*, 2nd edn. Oxford: Pergamon.

Reynolds, D. (1996) *Worlds Apart*. London: Ofsted.

Richardson, J. T. E. (1992) Cognitive psychology and student learning. *Psychology Teaching Review*, 1(1): 2–9.

Rowe, M. B. (1986) Wait-time: slowing down may be a way of speeding up! *Journal of Teacher Education*, 37: 43–50.

Rutkowska, J. C. (1993) *The Computational Infant: Looking for Developmental Cognitive Science*. New York: Harvester.

Schneider, W. (1994) Memory development, in T. Husen and T. N. Postlethwaite (eds) *International Encyclopedia of Education*, 2nd edn. Oxford: Pergamon.

Sharron, H. and Coulter, M. (1994) *Changing Children's Minds: Feuerstein's Revolution in the Teaching of Intelligence*. London: Sharron Publishing.

Simon, T. J. and Halford, G. S. (1995) *Developing Cognitive Competence: New Approaches to Process Modelling*. Hillsdale NJ: Lawrence Erlbaum.

Siraj-Blatchford, J. and Siraj-Blatchford, I. (eds) (1995) *Educating the Whole Child: Cross-Curricular Themes and Dimensions*. Buckingham: Open University Press.

Slavin, R. E. (1983) *Cooperative Learning*. London: Longman.

Smith, A. (1996) *Accelerated Learning in the Classroom*. Stafford: Network Educational Press.

Smith, P. K. (1993) Social development, in A. M. Colman (ed.) *Companion Encyclopedia of Psychology*, vol. 2, London: Routledge.

Sotto, E. (1994) *When Teaching Becomes Learning: a Theory and Practice of Teaching*. London: Cassell.

SRA (Science Research Associates) (1984) *Direct Instruction – a Review*. Henley-on Thames: Science Research Associates.

Stevenson, R. J. and Palmer, J. A. (1994) *Learning: Principles, Processes and Practices*. London: Cassell.

Stevick, E. W. (1996) *Memory, Meaning and Method*, 2nd edn. Boston MA: Heinle and Heinle.

Swan, S. and White, R. (1994) *The Thinking Books*. London: Falmer.

Teacher Training Agency (TTA) (1994) *Profiles of Competence: Draft Note of Guidance*. London: TTA.

Teacher Training Agency (TTA) (1997) *Standards for the Award of Qualified Teacher Status*. London: TTA.

Tharp, R. and Gallimore, R. (1991) A theory of teaching as assisted performance, in P. Light, S. Sheldon and M. Woodhead (eds) *Child Development in Social context 2: Learning to Think*. London: Routledge.

Thompson, M. (1992) Do 27 competencies make a teacher? Or, why chickens should decide the sauce in which they are to be served. *Education Review*, 6(2): 4–7.

Tizard, B. and Hughes, M. (1984) *Young Children Learning: Talking and Thinking at Home and at School*. London: Fontana.

Topping, K. J. and Wolfendale, S. (1985) *Parental Involvement in Children's Reading*. London: Croom Helm.

Tully, M. (1996) I was always a bolshie, *Times Educational Supplement*, 26 January: 24.

Wheldall, K., Merrett, F. and Glynn, T. (1986) *Behaviour Analysis in Educational Psychology*. Beckenham: Croom Helm.

Wilce, H. (1994) Spare the praise, save the child, *Times Educational Supplement*, 25 March: 16.

Wood, D. (1988) *How Children Think and Learn: the Social Contexts of Cognitive Development*. Oxford: Blackwell.

Wood, D. (1991) Aspects of teaching and learning, in P. Light, S. Sheldon and M. Woodhead (eds) *Child Development in Social Context 2: Learning to Think*. London: Routledge.

Woods, P. (1995) *Creative Teaching in Primary Schools*. Buckingham: Open University Press.

Yates, F. A. (1966) *The Art of Memory*. London: Routledge and Kegan Paul.

Index

STARTING FROM THE CHILD?
TEACHING AND LEARNING FROM 4 TO 8

Julie Fisher

Early years practitioners currently face a number of dilemmas when planning an education for young children. The imposition of an external curriculum seems to work in opposition to the principles of planning experiences which start from the child. Does this mean that the notion of a curriculum centred on the needs and interests of children is now more rhetoric than reality?

In a practical and realistic way *Starting from the Child?* examines a range of theories about young children as learners and the implications of these theories for classroom practice. Julie Fisher acknowledges the competence of young children when they arrive at school, the importance of building on their early successes and the critical role of adults who understand the individual and idiosyncratic ways of young learners. The book addresses the key issues of planning and assessment, explores the place of talk and play in the classroom and examines the role of the teacher in keeping a balance between the demands of the curriculum and the learning needs of the child.

This is essential reading, not only for early years practitioners, but for all those who manage and make decision about early learning.

Contents
Competent young learners – Conversations and observations – Planning for learning – The role of the teacher – Encouraging independence – Collaboration and cooperation – The place of play – The negotiated classroom – Planning, doing and reviewing – Evaluation and assessment – References – Index.

192pp   0 335 19556 3 (Paperback)   0 335 19557 1 (Hardback)

PRIMARY SCHOOLS AND THE FUTURE
CELEBRATION, CHALLENGES AND CHOICES

Patrick Whitaker

This book has two important purposes. The first is to consider the challenges facing primary schools as they move towards a new century and a new millennium.

The second purpose of the book is to celebrate the work of primary schools and to note their unique qualities and achievements. Within these two broad purposes are four specific aims:

- to examine the changed and changing circumstances within which primary school education is now set;
- to explore the unique organizational features of primary schools and their potential for dynamic development;
- to outline specific strategies to meet the challenges of the future;
- to consider the nature of the educational leadership that will be required.

The book provides clear, practical, inspiring guidance for those involved in primary school management and will be invaluable reading for all staff in primary schools.

Contents
Preface – The changing world – The paradigm shift – Achievement and potential – Learning and teaching – Culture and well-being – Getting things done – Teamwork and collaboration – Transformative leadership – Meeting the future – New millennium educators – Bibliography – Index.

192pp   0 335 19423 0 (Paperback)   0 335 19424 9 (Hardback)

ORGANIZING FOR LEARNING IN THE PRIMARY CLASSROOM
A BALANCED APPROACH TO CLASSROOM MANAGEMENT

Janet R. Moyles

What is it that underlies classroom organization, routines, rules, structures and daily occurrences? What are the prime objectives and what influences the decisions of teachers and children? What is it useful for teachers to consider when contemplating the issues of classroom management and organization? What do different practices have to offer?

Organizing for Learning in the Primary Classroom explores the whole range of influences and values which underpin *why* teachers do *what* they do in the classroom context and what these mean to children and others. Janet Moyles examines teaching and learning styles, children's independence and autonomy, coping with children's differences, the physical classroom context and resources, time management and ways of involving others in the day-to-day organization. Practical suggestions are given for considering both the functional and aesthetic aspects of the classroom context. Opportunities are provided for teachers to reflect on their own organization and also consider innovative and flexible ways forward to deal with new and ever increasing demands on their time and sanity!

This book is to be highly recommended for all primary school teachers . . .

(Management in Education)

. . . indispensable to courses in initial teacher education and to providers of inset.

(Child Education)

Janet Moyles brings her long experience of the primary school to *Organizing for Learning in the Primary Classroom* . . . I particularly like the attention she gives to the physical environment, giving lots of advice about arrangements of furniture and the role of the teacher's desk . . .

(Times Educational Supplement)

Contents

208pp   0 335 15659 2 (Paperback)   0 335 15660 6 (Hardback)